Crafty Cr

Snappy Snacks

Quick and Easy Snacks
for Young Cooks

Best Wishes
Liz Ashworth

Liz Ashworth

Scottish Children's Press

Commit your work to the Lord, then it will succeed
– Proverbs 16, verse 3

First published 2004 by

SCOTTISH CHILDREN'S PRESS
Unit 6, Newbattle Abbey Business Park
Newbattle Road, Dalkeith, EH22 3LJ, Scotland
Tel: +44 (0)131 660 4757 • Fax: +44 (0)131 660 4666
Email: info@scottishbooks.com
www.scottishbooks.com

Copyright © Liz Ashworth, 2004
Liz Ashworth has asserted her right under the Copyright,
Designs and Patents Act, 1988, to be identified as Author of this Work

Illustrations by Craig Ellery
Design by Avril Gray

All rights reserved. No part of this publication may be reproduced, stored in a retrieval system, or transmitted in any form or by any means, electronic, mechanical, photocopying, recording or otherwise, without the prior permission, in writing, of Scottish Children's Press

BRITISH LIBRARY CATALOGUING IN PUBLICATION DATA
A catalogue record for this book is available from the British Library

ISBN: 1 899827 18 8

Printed and bound by Cromwell Press, Trowbridge, Wiltshire

Contents

Also available:

Teach the Bairns to Bake
Traditional Scottish Baking for Beginners

ISBN: 1 899827 24 2

Teach the Bairns to Cook
Traditional Scottish Recipes for Beginners

ISBN: 1 899827 23 4

Teach the Bairns Vegetarian Cooking
Traditional Scottish Recipes for Beginners

ISBN: 1 899827 66 8

Please contact Scottish Children's Press for
further details or for a complete catalogue

www.scottishbooks.com

Introduction

One of the most important things is to have fun in the kitchen. If you enjoy yourself then it won't matter so much if your recipes don't turn out right the first time – you can have more fun as you make them all over again! Remember, even the best chefs burn dinner from time to time!

This book is aimed at everyone – from young children just learning to cook, to students leaving home for the first time, to busy office workers in need of something different for lunch. It is easy to follow and a lot of the recipes don't need to be cooked at all. Don't worry if you need to make a meal for someone on a special diet – you'll find lots of recipes in this book.

Thanks to my son and his friends for their dedication and valour in the face of numerous tasting and commenting sessions, and for writing the jokes which I just had to add to season the recipes.

Preparing and sharing food, no matter how simple, with family and friends is one of the most enjoyable things in life – get cooking and have fun together!

Liz Ashworth

IMPORTANT

Before You Begin to Cook

1 ALWAYS ask an adult if it is ok to cook in the kitchen. If you are not sure what to do, they can be a great help.

2 For safety in the kitchen:

- Tie back long hair (not so tasty in a snack!).
- Wear an apron or overall to protect your clothes.
- Do not wear open shoes or sandals in case anything hot falls on your toes.
- When you are stirring, mixing or beating, put a clean, damp cloth under the bowl to stop it from slipping.
- Use oven gloves or mitts on both hands to lift hot trays, dishes, tins or pans.

3 Decide on the recipe you would like to make and check how long it will take. Always read the recipe carefully right through before you start. Make sure you understand everything you have to do. Read through the list of ingredients and utensils again and set out everything you will need on the table before you start preparing the dish.

4 Wash and dry your hands, and all work surfaces, before you start.

5 Weigh all the ingredients carefully. If you do not have kitchen scales, you can buy inexpensive measuring spoons and scoops from hardware shops to measure the quantities easily.

6 Use a chopping board to chop food. Never hold a knife by its blade.

7 Open tins of food carefully. Some tins have a ring to pull and open. If you are using a tin opener or pulling the ring to open the tin, watch out for sharp edges! They can cause a nasty cut.

8 Set a minute timer if you are cooking – the beep will remind you to take your food off the hob or out of the oven before it burns!

9 Baking in the oven means you have to stay as watchful as a crocodile! Arrange the shelves in the oven as it says in the recipe. Then turn the oven on to heat at the right temperature – that way it will be ready to cook your snack as soon as you have made it.

10 Cooking on the hob also needs a careful eye. Always hold the handle of a pan when you are stirring or turning food. Make sure that the pot's handle is not sticking out from the hob and that it can't be knocked – you don't want your dinner to end up on the floor! More serious spills might mean that you badly burn yourself, so be safe. Be careful when you move the handle that you don't let it hang over the hot hob or it will get hot too and will burn your hands when you go to lift it.

11 Have a heat-resistant surface nearby to set hot tins and baking trays on. A wooden chopping board will do.

12 Remember to turn off the oven, hob, gas or electricity when you have finished using it.

Temperatures and Safety Tips

Your Oven

Check whether your oven is gas or electric. An electric oven can be measured in two ways:

- If your oven shows a temperature range from 0° to 550°, it is measured in degrees Fahrenheit = °F.
- If it shows a range from 0° to 250°, it is measured in degrees Celsius = °C.

The temperature of a fan oven is higher than that of a conventional oven. You will need to lower the temperature according to the manufacturer's instructions (usually 5°).

Be sure to read the recipe carefully and set your oven to the correct temperature.

GAS MARK	FAHRENHEIT	CENTIGRADE	TEMPERATURE
1	275°F	140°C	low
2	300°F	150°C	
3	325°F	170°C	fairly low
4	350°F	180°C	medium
5	375°F	190°C	
6	400°F	200°C	fairly hot
7	425°F	220°C	hot
8	450°F	230°C	very hot
9	475°F	240°C	

Oven shelves

Different recipes are baked in different parts of the oven. Arrange the shelves for the recipe **before** you turn on the oven. If you need to re-arrange the shelves, use oven gloves.

Pan sizes

saucepan – holds 1½–2 pints (1.25 litres) of water

stew pan – holds 3–4 pints (2.5 litres) of water

large soup pot – holds 5–6 pints (3.5 litres) of water

A 'double boiler'

Place a heat-proof bowl over, but not touching, hot water in a pan. Put the pan on a low heat. The steam from the water cooks, melts or softens the mixture (for example, chocolate) in the bowl.

Testing the temperature of fat or oil

Drop in a piece of dry bread to test the temperature of hot fat or oil (stand back so that the oil does not splash and burn you). If the bread bubbles and turns golden, the fat or oil is ready. If the bread burns, the fat is too hot. If the fat does not bubble it is too cold. **Be very careful** around boiling fat, hot oil or steam. Steam and cooking fat are very hot, hotter than boiling water, and can give you a very nasty burn.

If you burn yourself

- Call for an adult to come and help.

- If your skin is splashed with a hot liquid, or is touched by steam, or you accidentally touch a hot surface, put the affected area under cold running water as quickly as you can. This will take the heat out of the burn. You should keep it in the cold water for about 10 minutes. Remember, the quicker you get the burn into cold water the better chance you have of stopping it from blistering and causing scarring.

In Case of Fire

- Call an adult.
- Turn off the heat if it is **safe** to do so.
- Get away from the fire.
- Do **NOT** put water on it.

Preparing Fruit and Herbs

apples and pears

Wash under cold running water. Remove the skin with a
potato peeler. Place on a chopping board and slice the
fruit in half from top (stalk end) to bottom. Lay on its
flat side and cut in half again. Remove the core from
each quarter with a sharp knife. Use as soon as possible
– if you have to leave the fruit, place it in a bowl and
cover with cold water. Add a little lemon juice to prevent
the fruit turning brown.

gooseberries, blackcurrants and redcurrants

Use a pair of scissors to cut off the stalk and the dry
leafy part at the opposite end. This is called 'topping
and tailing'. Place in a sieve or colander and wash under
cold running water. Drain and use.

raspberries and blackberries

Remove the leaves and white inner core
with your thumb and forefinger. Put into
a colander and wash quickly but gently
(don't bruise the fruit) under cold
running water. Drain and use.

strawberries

Remove the leaves and white core using
a pair of sugar tongs or tweezers. Put
into a colander and wash under cold
running water. Drain and use.

Juicing fruit

Some very fancy machines exist which will do this job for you however, one of two simple pieces of kitchen equipment can do the job just the same.

a fork This is very useful for squeezing the juice out of citrus fruits like oranges, lemons, limes and grapefruit. Simply wash the fruit well, dry it and then cut through the middle to make two halves. Hold half in one hand over a bowl. Take a fork in your other hand and push it into the centre of the flesh of the fruit. While you are doing this, squeeze the fruit to force the juice into the bowl. Repeat with the other half.

You can also buy shaped wooden or plastic 'juicing sticks' which work the same way as a fork.

a juice squeezer These strange-looking things have a funny dome shaped part over which you place the halved fruit, flesh side down. Rub the fruit from side to side squeezing all the time and the juice will collect in the tray round the bottom.

Remember to strain the juice through a sieve to catch all the pips and other bits.

herbs

fresh herbs Wash under cold running water, drain well in a colander or sieve, and dry thoroughly in a clean tea towel or kitchen towel. Remove the tough stalks with a pair of kitchen scissors and cut into small pieces. (This is easier and safer than chopping small sprigs with a sharp knife.)

Some supermarkets sell herbs all ready washed – use what you want and freeze the rest in a poly bag for later. Look out for **frozen herbs** in your local supermarket as well.

dried herbs can be used instead of fresh herbs. Use half the quantity of dried herbs compared with fresh herbs.

Preparing Vegetables

avocado

Starting at the narrow pointed end, slide a sharp knife about halfway into the avocado and cut towards the fatter end. Ease the knife all the way round to the pointed end again. Twist the halves in opposite directions to pull them apart. To get the stone out of the middle, whack it with the blade of the knife (keeping fingers well out of the way), twist the stone and lift it out. Give the knife a hard tap on the side of the rubbish bin and the stone will fall off into the bin and not on to the floor! Avocado pears are a creamy green colour inside but they go brown very easily. Dip them in lemon juice to keep the green colour.

beetroot

Beetroot is a root vegetable with bright pink flesh. Wear rubber gloves to peel beetroot – cooked or raw – and keep the beetroot separate from other food, or you will find that hands and food turn pink too! Save time and buy ready cooked.

broccoli and cauliflower

Remove the outer leaves and cut away the thick stem – throw these away. Wash the vegetable under cold running water, place on a chopping board and cut the flower into smaller, even-sized flowers – called 'sprigs'. Place the sprigs in a clean pan or bowl and cover with cold water until you are ready to cook them. Just before cooking, drain off the water through a colander placed in the sink, and boil in fresh, salted water for about 8 minutes until tender.

cabbage, kail, etc. (green vegetables)

Prepare green vegetables just before you cook them so that they keep their goodness. Cut off the root, peel off any dead or tough outer leaves and throw them away. Wash under cold running water and drain in a colander. Place on a chopping board and use a sharp knife to cut off and throw away any thick stalks or stringy parts.

carrots, parsnips, potatoes (root vegetables)

Wash the vegetables under cold running water. Use a potato peeler or a sharp knife to peel off a thin skin. Cut out and throw away any bruised, discoloured or rotten pieces using the point of the knife or peeler. Cut into even sized pieces on a chopping board with a sharp knife. Place the pieces in a pan or bowl and cover with cold water until you are ready to use them.

To make carrot sticks: place the peeled and washed carrot on a chopping board and use a sharp knife to cut it in half lengthwise. Place each half flat side down on the chopping board and, holding the carrot steady with one hand, cut off long strips as thick or as thin as you like.

Potato varieties: Just as people are all different, there are many kinds of potatoes – some have a dry floury inside and others are a wetter, more waxy, consistency. They all cook differently too – some are good for salads, some should be roasted, some mashed and others baked. Most pre-packed potatoes tell you what they are best used for, so check the label.

celery

Celery comes in long stalks. Tear a stalk off the main (thickest) stem (called the celery heart). Hold it under cold running water and use a vegetable brush to scrub it clean.

leeks and spring onions

Place the leeks or spring onions on a chopping board and use a sharp knife to cut off the root. Remove any dead outer leaves. Trim off the tops and throw these away too. Wash under cold running water. **Leeks**: Cut the leeks in half lengthways and run the water inside to wash out any soil.

Spring Onions: Cut the stalks with a pair of scissors. Leeks and spring onions can be cut into different shapes. **Rings**: lay the stalks on a chopping board and cut across the lengths to make small rings. **Dice**: lay the stalks on the chopping board and cut along the length of the stalks to make strips, then cut across these to make small squares or 'dice'.

lettuce

There are lots of different kinds of lettuce in the shops – you can even buy bags of ready washed leaves. If you have a whole lettuce, place it on a chopping board and use a sharp knife to trim off the outer leaves and cut off the bottom of the stem. Put the lettuce into the sink and pull off the leaves one by one, holding each one under cold running water to wash it. Shake off the water and put the leaves in a sieve or colander to drain. Store in a poly bag in the bottom of the fridge to keep fresh for up to 3 days.

onions

Place the onion on a chopping board and use a sharp knife to cut off the root and stalk ends. Remove the papery outer skin. **To slice the onion**: *cut it in half from top to bottom. Lay one half of the onion on its flat side. Hold it with one hand and cut it into thin slices from top to bottom. Do the same with the other half.* **To chop the onion**: *slice the onion (see above) then cut across the slices to make small squares. My friend wears swimming goggles to stop her from crying and it works!*

peppers

Wash the pepper in cold running water, dry with kitchen towel and place on the chopping board. Use the sharp knife to cut round the green stalk and core to remove them. You will find that the core leaves behind lots of little seeds – remove all these from the inside of the pepper with a teaspoon. **To slice the pepper**: *cut it in half from top to bottom. Lay one half of the pepper on its flat side. Hold it with one hand and cut it into thin slices from top to bottom. Do the same with the other half.* **To chop the pepper**: *slice the pepper (see above) then cut across the slices to make small squares. Peppers can be eaten raw or cooked.*

rhubarb

Rhubarb is a vegetable which we use like a fruit! Place on a chopping board and use a sharp knife to remove the leaves and bottom of the stem. Wash under cold running water and dry with a clean tea towel. On a clean chopping board, cut across the stalks to make chunks.

tomatoes

Wash and dry tomatoes, and remove the green stalk. Place the tomatoes on a chopping board and use a sharp knife to slice each tomato in half from top (stalk end) to bottom. Cut a little 'v' shape round the hard piece of stalk on each half of the tomato, remove it and throw it away. **To make slices**: lay the tomato on its flat side and holding it steady with one hand cut into slices across the tomato. **To dice the tomato**: cut across the slices to make little squares. **To quarter for salads**: cut in half through the stalk, cut out the little 'v' shape then cut each piece of tomato in half again.

turnips and swedes

Turnips and swedes have a thick skin. Peel it off with a sharp knife. Cut out and throw away any bruised, discoloured or rotten pieces. Cut into even sized pieces on a chopping board with a sharp knife. Place the pieces in a bowl or pan and cover with water until you are ready to use them.

Cooking Fruit and Vegetables

Boiling

Drain any water used to soak the vegetables by tipping them into a colander in the sink. Place the vegetables in a pan and cover with boiling water. Add a pinch of salt (2 level teaspoons for potatoes) and bring to the boil on a high heat. Reduce the heat until the vegetables are simmering, put the lid on the pan and cook until tender. Root vegetables take 10 to 20 minutes, leaves take 5 minutes – see below for how to test to make sure they are cooked.

Steaming

Drain any water used to soak the vegetables by tipping them into a colander in the sink. Pour enough boiling water into the bottom of the steamer to reach halfway up the side. Place the vegetables in the top part of the steamer and put on the lid. Cook on a low to medium heat until the vegetables are tender. The time this takes depends on the size, age and type of vegetable. See below for how to test to make sure they are cooked.

Testing cooked fruit or vegetables

Use the point of a sharp knife or skewer to test that fruit or vegetables are cooked. Push the point into the flesh and if it goes all the way through easily, the fruit or vegetables are cooked.

Draining

Place a colander in the sink. Using oven gloves, remove the lid from the pan and tip the vegetables and water into the colander to drain. Keep your face away from the hot steam which could burn you. Run cold water into the sink to help stop the steam from filling the kitchen.

Simple Spoonfuls

'Level' and 'rounded'

Take a knife and smooth the amount on the top of the spoon so that it is flat – this is called a 'level spoonful', sometimes called a 'half spoonful'.

One level teaspoon = half a teaspoon

One level tablespoon = ½oz = 12.5g

When an amount of, say, flour is described as 'rounded', there is as much flour on the top of the spoon as the shape of the spoon below.

One rounded teaspoon = 1 teaspoonful = 5ml

One rounded tablespoon of flour = 1oz = 25g

One tablespoon of liquid = 1 fl.oz = 15ml

Spoon sizes

A dessertspoon is a spoon which is bigger than a teaspoon but smaller than a tablespoon.

One rounded tablespoon = 1oz

One rounded dessertspoon = ½oz

One rounded teaspoon = ¼oz

Recipe short hand

In the recipes, Crafty Croc uses a short way of writing spoons:

tsp = teaspoon

tbsp = tablespoon

Easy Eggs

Breaking eggs

Never break an egg directly into food in case the egg is bad and you will have to throw everything away. Test the egg first:

1 Hold the egg over a cup and tap the middle of the shell with a knife to crack it.

2 Open the shell with your thumbs and let the inside of the egg drop into the cup.

3 Check its smell and colour. If it smells or looks funny then chuck it away – if in doubt, throw it out!

4 If the recipe needs more than one egg, always break them into a cup one at a time and then add to a bowl for mixing. This means that you can throw out one which may not be fresh before it is mixed with the others.

Two ways to separate egg yolk and white

1 **Use an egg separator**: an egg separator is like a small round flat cup with a slit in the side of it. Separating an egg in this is like trying to control a hyper-active jelly fish! Hold the separator over a bowl and break the egg into the cup; the egg white will run out of the slit into the bowl, leaving the egg yolk in the cup.

2 **Use the eggshell**: wash and dry the egg very carefully. Break it into a cup or bowl. Take half of the clean eggshell and carefully cut into the egg white with the sharp shell and lift out the yolk. Eggshell is more effective than a spoon because the sharpness of the shell cuts away the white sticking to the yolk and makes it easier to lift out. It is perfect for lifting out any small broken pieces of eggshell.

Sugar Sense

Keep that happy smile!

The recipes in this book are all delicious, and they can all be healthy too. Part of taking care of what you put in your body is looking after your teeth. They have to last you all of your life. You can keep your teeth looking and feeling good by not snacking on sugary foods between meals – this is the time when sugar can do the most damage to your teeth.

If you do have a sugary snack then brush your teeth afterwards because the sugar can turn into acid called plaque which attacks the enamel (the white shiny stuff) and eventually eats holes in your teeth.

Crafty Croc's toothy tips

1 Brush your teeth well for 2 minutes twice a day with a toothpaste which contains fluoride, which helps to keep teeth strong and healthy.

2 Floss your teeth regularly as this will clean out any plaque which might be starting to form in between your teeth.

3 Change your toothbrush every two or three months to make sure you have the best equipment for the job.

4 Try not to eat too many sweets. When you do eat sweets, have them after a meal, or brush your teeth afterwards to get rid of the sugar. If you can't brush your teeth after eating sweets, then:

   a) chew a piece of dental chewing gum or

   b) eat a piece of cheese – this helps remove the sugar

5 Visit your dentist regularly, to **avoid** a filling!

Simple Cooking Terms

Batter A mix of flour, eggs and liquid. The thickness of the batter depends on what it is to be used to make. A batter which will coat the food is the thickness of double cream.

Beat To stir food fast. Use a spoon, whisk or electric beater.

Blend To use a liquidiser, blender or sieve and spoon to make something smooth in consistency and remove all the lumps (for example, in soups and sauces).

Boil To cook food over a high heat so that the liquid moves; bubbles appear and steam rises from it.

Chop To cut food into small pieces. To chop something finely is to cut it up as small as you can.

Cream To beat butter (or margarine) and sugar until the mixture becomes light and fluffy.

Dough Dough is a mixture of flour (or meal) and a liquid. It is stiff and elastic like Play Dough. The stiffness depends on the food you are making.

Egg wash Also called 'egg glaze'. To paint the top of dough or pastry with beaten egg to give a golden shiny top when baked.

Dice To cut food into small equal sized cubes.

Drain To pour off the liquid which you don't need. You usually use a colander or a sieve which is placed over the sink or (if you need to save the liquid) a bowl.

Folding in To very gently mix two or more ingredients together. Using a tablespoon the mixture is lifted and mixed with light strokes. This mixing method is used so that the air in the mixture is not knocked out by stirring too much.

Grate To rub food against a grater to make crumbs or fine shreds. To grate citrus rind: wash the fruit well, put the grater on a plate and rub the skin on the rough dimpled part of the grater until you have rubbed off the coloured waxy outer surface of the skin – do not rub into the white part called 'pith' which has a bitter taste. Use a knife to scrape all the peel off the grater.

Grease	To rub something, for example a baking dish or tray, with butter, margarine or oil. This stops the food from sticking to it.
Knead	To mix dough together using both hands. On a floured surface, push the dough down and away from you while squeezing it together. Still squeezing, pull the dough back towards you, then push it down and away again. Do this until the dough is smooth and mixed.
Marinate	To soak food in a mixture called a 'marinade' which will add flavour and tenderise the food before cooking.
Pinch	A pinch is the amount you can hold between your thumb and forefinger (pointing finger).
Shred	To cut food, like cabbage, into very thin small strips.
Sieve	To rub flour and other dry ingredients through a sieve placed over a mixing bowl. Use the back of a tablespoon to push everything through the sieve. This removes any lumps or dirt and adds air to your baking.
Simmer	To cook food over a low heat so that it bubbles now and again.
Slice	To cut food into thin, flat portions.
Soak	To cover an ingredient with liquid (usually water, milk, fruit juice or oil) and leave for a period of time (a few hours or overnight). Food is soaked to soften it, to remove impurities or to allow the liquid to be absorbed.
Stir	To mix ingredients together with a spoon or fork until they are all well blended together.
Sweating	To cook very slowly in a little oil, margarine or butter until soft.
Tasting	To eat a tiny amount of the food you are cooking to check the seasoning or sweetness so that you can add salt, pepper or sugar as required to make the flavour better. Dip a spoon into the food you are tasting and drop some on to your spoon. Never put the spoon which has been in your mouth back into the food.
Whip	To beat a liquid with a whisk. Egg whites will become light and frothy, but do not overbeat them or they will become liquid again. Cream will become thick. Take care not to overbeat or it will turn into butter.

Special Diets

If you are allergic to certain foods or just don't eat them, it can be hard to find tasty treats. If you are friends with someone who is on a special diet and has to avoid eating things like nuts, fish, meat, dairy products like cheese or milk, wheat, or even sugar, it can be hard too. These recipes are specially created to make it easier to plan parties, picnics and packed lunches which everyone can enjoy. And they are not hard to make!

Special diet alternatives *have been placed in brackets. This means that you can change the recipe to suit other diets. For example, sometimes you can swop one ingredient with another to make the recipe ok for someone on a Dairy Free diet. Find out if your friends or family have special diet needs, then always:*

- *carefully check the list of ingredients on all tins, packets, jars and tubs of food to see if they are suitable for the people who are going to eat the food you make*

- *read the recipe carefully to make sure that you have not over-looked anything.*

Healthy options *have also been placed in brackets. This allows you to see and follow the healthy option, but means that you can still make the recipe if you only have the higher fat ingredients. When you are buying your ingredients and planning meals try and use:*

- *semi-skimmed milk*

- *half-fat cheddar, gouda or edam cheese*

- *reduced-sugar, high-fruit jam.*

Diabetic (DB)

A diabetic needs to eat good wholesome food at regular times to keep their body going. The 'GI index' is a huge help when looking for foods that are good for diabetics to eat – find this on the internet (key in 'glycemic index'). Low GI foods are best for diabetics – see how many you can find.

Dairy Free (DF)

For various reasons, drinking milk (cows' milk and sometimes goats' and sheep's milk too) along with all the other things made with milk (like cheese, yoghurt, cream and so on) make some people feel unwell. Sometimes a Dairy Free diet means no eggs! Some people cannot eat egg white, while others cannot eat egg yolk. It is always best to be safe and ask them.

Gluten Free (GF)

Gluten is the starch that makes flour stretchy and sticky when it's made into doughs for bread, biscuits, cakes and pancakes. It is a protein found in wheat, barley, oats and rye and can make some people unwell. Gluten Free flour is made from flours like rice, buckwheat and maize which do not contain gluten. You can buy gluten free wheat – but this is NOT suitable for a Wheat Free diet.

Wheat Free (WF)

Some people find that eating wheat makes them unwell, however this does not mean that they need a Gluten Free diet – they will probably be able to eat barley, oats and rye flours instead. It is always best to be safe and ask them.

Vegan (V)

This is someone who has decided for health or other reasons not to eat anything connected with a living thing. They eat a diet which contains purely vegetable foods like peas, beans, lentils, lots of vegetables and grains like wheat, oats, barley, rye, rice, millet, maize, soya and many others besides.

Vegetarian (VG)

A vegetarian is someone who has decided for health or other reasons to live only on vegetable food. Most Vegetarians eat dairy products, honey and eggs, but some do not. Food labels use the symbol 'VG' to tell you that there are no meat products in the food. 'V' means that there are no dairy products, honey or eggs in the food either.

Key

     simple, straightforward recipe

     will require some help

   will need supervision and help
throughout this recipe

Takes 1 hour 20 mins   the recipe will take one hour and
20 minutes to make (this time will
change for each recipe)

No Cooking   no cooking required

Cook   needs cooking

Hob   uses the hob

Grill   uses the grill

Oven   uses the oven

Microwave   uses the microwave

Freeze   the recipe has to be frozen

DB   suitable for diabetics

DF   a dairy free recipe

GF   a gluten free recipe

V   suitable for vegans

VG   suitable for vegetarians

WF   a wheat free recipe

Note: where these symbols are shown in brackets,
you need to adapt the recipe to suit that specific diet.

Bread is Best!

If you are stuck for an idea, grab some bread, which you probably have in the house anyway.

Be adventurous – go for Granary, Turkish, Sesame or even Sun-dried Tomato bread. All the snacks in this chapter can be made with Gluten Free or Wheat Free breads when you see (GF) or (WF) in the key.

Snappy sandwiches make très bons snacks !

NighTmaRe

in the Kitchen

Serves 1

Takes 10 mins

Cook – grill (or sandwich toaster or toaster bag)

DB

(GF)

VG

(WF)

This is a sensational concoction featuring 'Stringy Flesh' and 'Hot Red Monster Blood'!

Crunchy carrot sticks taste good with this (see page 13). Toaster bags are handy for this recipe – pop them in your toaster and cook. Easy!

Now to prepare
Eat it if you DARE!

You Will Need

2 thick slices of bread (try malted grain)
50g (2oz) edam, jarlsberg (or half-fat cheddar)
tomato ketchup (low sugar)
sunflower oil

chopping board
knife for spreading
teacup
pastry brush
fish slice
plate
oven gloves

Snap To It!

1 Place the bread on the chopping board. Use the knife to spread one side of one slice of bread with tomato ketchup.

2 Cover the ketchup with all of the sliced cheese.

3 Lay the other slice of bread on top to make a sandwich.

4 Pour a little sunflower oil into the teacup. Then use the pastry brush to paint the top of the sandwich very lightly with the oil.

5 Turn the sandwich over and paint the other slice of bread. The oil will make the bread turn golden and crisp when it is cooked.

6 Now choose how you cook your sandwich.

IN A SANDWICH TOASTER

a) Turn on the toaster to heat. Then carefully place the sandwich in the toaster using the fish slice.

b) Set your plate beside the sandwich toaster. When your sandwich is cooked, use the fish slice to place it on the plate.

UNDER THE GRILL

a) Turn the grill on to heat. Put on the oven gloves and, using the fish slice, carefully place the sandwich on the grill pan under the hot grill.

b) After a few minutes, when the top of the sandwich looks golden, carefully turn the sandwich over with the fish slice to grill the other side. Remember to wear the oven gloves.

c) Set your plate beside the grill. In 2 or 3 minutes your sandwich will be cooked. Use the fish slice to place it on the plate.

IN A TOASTER BAG

a) Carefully place the sandwich in the toaster bag.

b) Put the bag in the toaster and cook on high until it pops up again.

c) Set your plate beside the toaster. When your sandwich is cooked, use the oven gloves to lift it on to the plate.

7 Cut the sandwich in two and serve. Hey presto! – stringy flesh and red monster blood!!! Mmmm!

Fireman's Egg Sandwich

Serves 2

Takes 10 mins

Cook – hob

DB

(GF)

VG

(WF)

What is yellow and travels at 60 miles an hour?
– A Fireman's Egg Sandwich!

This recipe is guaranteed to stand the 'Fire Alarm and Fireman's Pole Test'! It will even stick together while you run down stairs – try it and see!

You Will Need

4 slices of bread (try wholemeal)
1 large egg
2 heaped tsp natural yoghurt (or fromage frais)
sunflower spread
salt + pepper

saucepan
bowl
grater
teaspoon
wooden spoon
chopping board
knife for spreading

Snap To It!

1. Place the egg into the pan and pour in enough water to cover it. Turn up the heat and let the egg boil for 8 minutes. Turn off the heat.

   To cool your egg quickly:

   Lift the pan into the sink and run cold water into it for a few minutes.

2. When the egg is cold, take it out of the pan and roll it along the table to crack the shell. Peel off the shell and wash the egg under cold running water.

3. Using the grater, very carefully grate the hard-boiled egg into the bowl.

4. Add the natural yoghurt (or fromage frais), salt and pepper and mix well together with the wooden spoon.

5. Spread one side of each slice of bread with sunflower spread.

6. Divide the egg mixture evenly between two slices of bread and use the knife to spread the mixture over the bread.

7. Place the other slices of bread on top (spread side down) to make two sandwiches. Use the palm of your hand to press the sandwiches well together – you don't want the filling to fall out if you are called to drive the fire engine!

8. Place the sandwiches on to the chopping board and use the knife to cut off the crusts and then into handy triangles.

9. Serve. Fireman's Egg Sandwich are very good to eat with some little cherry tomatoes – you can slip these into your pocket if the siren goes!

Be a Crafty Croc

You can buy ready-made egg mayonnaise in your local supermarket which means you can make this sandwich in a SNAP!

Ravenous Rabbit's
REVENGE

A cheeky rabbit has sneaked into the garden again and all the tender young lettuce and juicy carrots have disappeared – down his throat!

Quickly, make your sandwich while he is not looking – eat it all up before he tries to eat it too!

You Will Need

2 thick slices of bread (try granary)
2 crisp lettuce leaves (iceberg or cos lettuce)
1 small juicy carrot
25g (1oz) cheddar cheese
sunflower spread (dairy free)
1 tsp of sandwich pickle (or chutney)

chopping board
grater
bowl
sharp knife
knife for spreading
wooden spoon
potato peeler
teaspoon

Snap To It !

1 Use the roughest side of the grater to grate the cheese into the bowl. Be careful of your fingers, as the grater can be very sharp.

2 Wash the carrot with cold running water and peel with the potato peeler. Carefully, grate the carrot into the bowl. You can munch that last little piece of carrot!

3 Place the lettuce leaves on the chopping board and very carefully cut them up with the sharp knife into very thin strips – these are called 'shreds' (see page 21). Put them into the bowl too.

4 Mix everything together with the wooden spoon.

5 Add a teaspoon of pickle (or chutney) if you like it.

6 Wipe and dry the chopping board.

7 Lay the two slices of bread on the chopping board and spread the top of each with the sunflower spread.

8 Pile the filling on top of one slice and then cover with the other slice to make a sandwich. There's a lot of filling! Press it down with the flat palm of your hand and quickly cut your sandwich into two triangles.

9 Serve. It is best to eat this sandwich when you make it so that it is crisp and juicy – just the way the cheeky rabbit likes it.

Be a Crafty Croc

To turn this into a **Dairy Free** version, just leave out the cheese and use sultanas and sunflower seeds instead. Sultanas taste lovely with grated carrot!

Terrific Tower of Brain Power

Serves 1

Takes 10 mins

No cooking

DB

DF

(GF)

(WF)

Do you know that certain foods can make your brain work better? Tests have shown that if you eat tuna before an exam, it increases your concentration and helps you to think more clearly!

This Tower is good to eat at any time – and especially when extra 'Brain Power' is essential!

You Will Need

2 thick slices of brown bread (try wholemeal)
1 thick slice of white bread
sunflower spread (dairy free)
1 small tin of tuna in brine (or in spring water)
2 tsp tomato ketchup (or salad cream)
1 small ring of pineapple
2 crisp lettuce leaves

chopping board
tin opener
sieve
plate
sharp knife
knife for spreading
fork
bowl
teaspoon
4 long wooden cocktail sticks

Snap To It!

1 Place the ring of pineapple on the plate and carefully chop up into small pieces with a sharp knife.

2 Lay the lettuce leaves on the chopping board and cut them up with the sharp knife into very thin strips – these are called 'shreds'.

3 Open the tin of tuna with the tin opener, being careful of the sharp edges. Hold the sieve over the sink and tip the tuna into the sieve to drain off the water.

4 Put the tuna into the bowl.

5 Add the ketchup or salad cream (whichever you like best) to the tuna. Mix everything together using the fork.

6 Wipe and dry the chopping board. Place the brown bread on the chopping board and spread one side of each slice with the sunflower spread.

7 Pile the tuna filling on one slice and then place a slice of white bread on top.

8 Now pile the shredded lettuce and chopped pineapple on to the white bread.

9 Lastly, lay the slice of brown bread (spread side down) on top to make a tower.

10 Now for the exciting bit! To make 4 towers, cut your sandwich into quarters with the sharp knife. Be quick and stab a cocktail stick through each quarter as soon as you cut it.

11 Carefully lift each tower on to a plate and serve. You can make an even higher tower by piling other goodies on top – try cherry tomatoes, cucumber, pieces of pepper and even slices of radish!

Now, snap up the sandwich and feed your brain!

Skunk Sandwich

A special treat made with Smoked Skunk and Groovy Green Frog's Skin!

What do you get when you breed a skunk and a boomerang together?

A smell that just will not go away!

You Will Need

2 thick slices of bread (try soft grain)
3 rashers smoked bacon (or 3 slices of ham)
2 crisp lettuce leaves
1 avocado
1 medium tomato
sunflower spread (dairy free)

frying pan
fish slice
plate
kitchen towel
chopping board
knife for spreading
sharp knife
2 wooden cocktail sticks

Snap To It!

1 Lay the kitchen towel on the plate and place it beside the hob.

2 Place the frying pan on the hob and turn on the heat to medium. Place the bacon on the pan and fry the bacon for a few minutes on one side. Carefully, turn the bacon with a fish slice to fry the other side.

3 Turn off the heat. Use the fish slice to lift the bacon on to the kitchen towel. Carefully dry off all the extra fat from the bacon.

4 Spread one side of each slice of bread with the sunflower spread.

5 Place the lettuce on the chopping board and cut it up with the sharp knife into very thin strips – these are called 'shreds'.

6 Scatter the lettuce shreds over one slice of bread.

7 Break the bacon into pieces over the lettuce.

8 Place the tomato on the chopping board and use the sharp knife to cut it in half. Take one half, place the flat side down and carefully cut it into slices. Do the same with the other half.

9 Prepare the avocado (see page 12), place it on the chopping board and carefully slice it with the sharp knife.

10 Lay the slices of tomato and avocado on the lettuce and cover with the other slice of bread (spread side down). Press down gently with the palm of your hand.

11 Use the cocktail sticks to keep the sandwich together while you cut your sandwich into two neat triangles. Serve immediately.

Be a Crafty Croc

Eat your Skunk Sandwich as soon as you make it, otherwise the avocado will begin to turn a funny colour. Stop this happening by squeezing a little lemon juice on to the avocado slices before you make the sandwich.

Vegetarians and **Vegans** – use crunchy sunflower seeds instead of bacon.

Snappy Sputnik

All your friends will want to try this daring space-age sandwich.

Crunch through the walls of the space odyssey ship to the groovy filling within! Just like a spaceman, however, you will have to make your preparations before you can enjoy the spaceship!

Serves 2

Takes 15 mins

No cooking

DB

(DF)

(GF)

(VG)

(WF)

You Will Need

2 crisp fresh dinner rolls
1 small tin of pilchards in tomato sauce
1 small tin sweetcorn – drained
2 crisp lettuce leaves (try iceberg)
1 medium carrot
2 sticks of celery
1 tbsp set natural yoghurt
½ level tsp mild chilli powder

sieve
bowl
tin opener
fork
chopping board
bread knife
sharp knife
2 plates
teaspoon
2 serving plates

Snap To It!

1 Carefully open the tins of sweetcorn and pilchards (see page 7).

2 Hold the sieve over the sink and pour the sweetcorn into the sieve to drain it. Tip the drained sweetcorn into a bowl.

3 Add the pilchards, yoghurt and chilli powder to the sweetcorn. Mash them all together with a fork to make the filling.

4 Wash and dry the sticks of celery and place them on the chopping board. Use the sharp knife to carefully cut along the length of celery. Place the flat side face down on the board and slice along the length again. Do this a few more times so that you have long, thin strips of celery. Cut the other stick of celery in the same way. Place the pieces on a plate.

5 Wash, peel and dry the carrot. Slice it in the same way as you did the celery and put it on a clean plate.

6 Place the lettuce leaves on the chopping board and carefully cut them up with the sharp knife into thin strips – these are called 'shreds' (see page 21). Lay them on the two serving plates.

7 Now get your spaceship ready for take-off! Put the dinner rolls on the chopping board and carefully cut off the tops with the bread knife – these pieces will be the lids. Use the teaspoon to scoop out the filling from the main piece to make a hollow pot.

8 Sit one dinner roll pot on each plate of lettuce. Put a little lettuce into the bottom of each pot.

9 Divide the filling between the rolls.

10 Stick sticks of carrot and celery into the filling so that they stick out the sides like arms and then put the lid on top.

11 Serve. Do you know what a sputnik is or was? Enjoy yours.

Be a Crafty Croc

- To make this a **Dairy Free** snack, use soya yoghurt instead of natural yoghurt.
- **Vegetarians** can use humus instead of pilchards.

Fat Old Slipper

Serves 2

Takes 15 mins

No cooking

DB

DF

V

VG

Look for ciabatta bread to make this tasty treat – ciabatta is a type of Italian bread and translated into English means – 'Old Slipper'!!

Most supermarkets now sell loaves and rolls made with the ciabatta dough which is different to our bread and worth a chew!

You Will Need

2 ciabatta bread rolls
(or 1 small loaf cut into 2 pieces)
1 tub of humus
cucumber
2 spring onions – chopped
1 firm eating apple – Granny Smiths

chopping board
bread knife
knife for spreading
sharp knife
kitchen scissors

Snap To It!

1 Lay the ciabatta roll on the chopping board and carefully cut along the length with the bread knife.

2 Do the same with the other roll.

3 Open the bread out flat and spread humus on to the bottom half of each roll using the spreading knife.

4 Cut the spring onions with the scissors so that they drop all over the humus.

5 Place the cucumber on the chopping board and carefully cut off 4 or 5 slices. Place these on top of the spring onion.

6 Wash and dry the apple.

7 Place the apple on the chopping board. Use the sharp knife to cut it in half, from top to bottom.

8 Cut the halves in two along their lengths to make four quarters.

9 Cut round the core to remove it. Then carefully slice the quarters into neat slices.

10 Lay the apple slices on top of the cucumber and put the other half of ciabatta on the top. Press down on the lid to keep the filling from falling out.

11 Snap it up smartish! Tastier than real slippers!!

Be a Crafty Croc

Fat Old Slippers go down easier with a lovely cool drink. Wash yours down with a Woosh (see page 107)!

Tiddler Toasties

Serves 2

Takes 10 mins

Cook –
sandwich
toaster

DB

(DF)

(GF)

(WF)

Oily fish is good for you, it helps to keep you healthy. As you can imagine, Crafty Croc is very fond of fish too!

There are lots of fillings you can put in a toasted sandwich. Go to page 88 for a list of ideas, or make up your own!

You Will Need

4 slices of bread (try malted grain)
small tin of sardines in tomato sauce
50g (2oz) edam (or cheddar cheese)
2 spring onions
sunflower spread (dairy free)
1 packet of mustard cress
(or you can use lettuce)

sandwich toaster
chopping board
small bowl
food tongs or fish slice
knife for spreading
fork
tin opener
grater
2 plates
kitchen scissors
oven gloves

Snap To It!

1 Spread the sunflower spread on one side of each slice of bread.

2 Use the roughest side of the grater to grate the cheese into the bowl. Be careful of your fingers, as the grater can be very sharp.

3 Carefully open the tin of sardines with the tin opener. Some tins have a ring to pull and open. Watch out for sharp edges! Empty the sardines into the small bowl.

4 Using the scissors, cut the spring onions into the bowl and mash together with the fork.

5 Turn on the sandwich toaster to heat at medium and set two plates beside it.

6 Place two slices of bread, spread side down, on the chopping board.

7 Divide the fishy filling between the two slices.

8 Sprinkle over the grated cheese and then set the other two slices on bread on top, with the spread side out. The spread side will cook in the sandwich toaster and will make the outside of your sandwich golden and crispy.

9 Using oven gloves, open the sandwich toaster. Then use the tongs or fish slice to lift the sandwiches into the toaster. Remember, you have been heating the toaster so it will be very hot. Close the lid with the oven gloves.

10 Leave to cook for a few minutes until golden and crisp. Use oven gloves to open the sandwich toaster. 'Fish out' your Tiddler Toasties with tongs or fish slice and set them on the two plates.

11 These are hot! So use a knife to cut them and leave them to cool a bit. Serve with a bunch of cress or a few cherry tomatoes beside each sandwich.

Be a Crafty Croc

Leave out the cheese and use a dairy-free spread for a **Dairy Free** recipe.

Bulging Biceps!

Giant baps fill my empty tummy so well
and I just love the concoctions you can put
into them – try this one for size when you
are especially hungry.

This recipe will start you off and then
you can think of your own fillings.
Go to pages 90 to 92 for more ideas.

You Will Need

2 large baps
(choose from French crusty, granary or soft and
floury – sometimes called a Glasgow Roll)

1 apple
1 sweet young carrot
1 stick celery
1 tub taramasalata (or cottage cheese)
1 handful of juicy raisins (or sultanas or dates)
spicy chicken pieces (or chopped pineapple)

chopping board
bread knife
wooden spoon
sharp knife
potato peeler
spoon
bowl
grater
plate

Snap To It !

1 Using the potato peeler, peel the apple. Place it on the chopping board and carefully cut it into four pieces using the sharp knife. Then carefully cut out the core from each quarter.

2 Use the roughest side of the grater to grate each apple quarter into the bowl. Be careful of your fingers, as the grater can be very sharp.

3 Use a spoon to scrape off all the apple from the grater.

4 Wash the carrot and peel with the potato peeler.

5 Use the roughest side of the grater to grate the carrot into the bowl. Be careful of your fingers, as the grater can be very sharp.

6 Wash the celery and place it on the chopping board. Use the sharp knife to cut it into 2cm (1 inch) chunks. Add these pieces to the bowl.

7 Add the raisins, taramasalata and chicken pieces.

8 Mix well with the wooden spoon.

9 Wash and dry the chopping board. Place the baps on the board and then carefully cut across the middle of each one with the bread knife.

10 Divide the filling between the two bottom halves and set the other half on top to make a 'lid'.

11 Serve on a plate and enjoy.

Be a Crafty Croc

- If you are a lazy croc, use a tub of ready-made salad.
- Use special bread for **Wheat** and **Gluten Free** diets and, if you are buying a ready-made salad, check that the ingredients do not contain wheat. Watch out for pasta pieces and sauces which have flour in them!
- Don't use taramasalata or chicken pieces for **vegetarians** – try humus, it tastes wonderful!

Tantalising Torpedo – pizza style!

Serves 2

Takes 30 mins

Cook – grill

DB

(GF)

VG

(WF)

As long as you have cheese, you can make a Torpedo! This is a perfect Crafty Croc recipe as you can mix and match ingredients to suit yourself! Try this pizza Torpedo and then see page 46 for another idea. Have you any better recipes? Your own always taste best!

You Will Need

1 medium sized baguette (called a French Stick)
110g (4oz) cheese
(edam, cheddar or mozzarella is best)
1 large tomato
1 small tin of sweetcorn

tin opener
sharp knife
chopping board
baking tray
small bowl
bread knife
spoon
fork
fish slice or food tongs
sieve
grater
oven gloves
3 plates

Snap To It!

1   Place the tomato on the chopping board and use the sharp knife to cut it in half. Take one half, place the flat side down and carefully cut it into slices. Then cut across these slices to make small squares.

2   Do the same with the other tomato half. Then put the chopped tomato into the bowl.

3   Wash and dry the chopping board.

4   Open the tin of sweetcorn with the tin opener, being careful of the sharp edges. Hold the sieve over the sink and pour the sweetcorn into the sieve to drain away the liquid.

5   Add the sweetcorn to the tomatoes and mix with the fork.

6   Use the roughest side of the grater to grate the cheese on to one of the plates. Be careful of your fingers, as the grater can be very sharp.

7   Put the baguette on the board and carefully cut across it in half with the bread knife. Now, very carefully slice along the length of bread. Do the same with the other half so that you have four long flat pieces.

8   Use the spoon to divide the tomato and sweetcorn mixture between the four slices of baguette. Spread it out to the edges.

9   Sprinkle the cheese over the top.

10   Turn on the grill to heat at medium.

11   Place the four baguette pieces, cheese side up, on the baking tray. Put on the oven gloves and place the baking tray under the grill. You must watch your baguettes all the time so keep your oven gloves on. As soon as the cheese begins to melt, bubble and turn golden, whisk the baking tray out and place it on a heat-resistant surface.

12   Use the tongs or fish slice to lift the Torpedoes on to two plates and serve. Mamma mia! This tastes great!

French Fancy

Serves 4

Takes 30 mins

Cook – grill

DB

(DF)

(GF)

(VG)

(WF)

Did you know that French Bread is made in a special way and is only nice to eat the day you buy it. In fact, in France people often buy fresh bread from the baker for each meal as it goes hard very quickly.

The bakers are open every day to make bread – even on Sundays and Christmas Day!

You Will Need

1 small baguette (called a French Stick)
165g (6oz) sliced edam or jarlsberg cheese
2 large tomatoes
110g (4oz) chopped cooked chicken (or tuna fish)
1 tbsp mayonnaise (low fat)
crunchy carrot sticks – if you like

chopping board
sharp knife
bread knife
baking tray
fish slice or food tongs
knife for spreading
bowl
tablespoon
oven gloves

Snap To It!

1 Lay the baguette on the chopping board and then cut in half across the centre with the bread knife.

2 Carefully cut along each length with the bread knife.

3 Lay the bread quarters on the baking tray, crusts facing down.

4 Place one tomato on the chopping board and use the sharp knife to slice it in half. Keep slicing the pieces in half until you have small squares.

5 Do the same with the other tomato and put all the chopped tomato into the bowl.

6 Add the chicken (or tuna) and mix in the mayonnaise.

7 Spoon the mixture equally on to the four flat open pieces of bread and spread it all over with the spreading knife.

8 Turn on the grill to heat at high.

9 Cover the chicken and tomato mixture with slices of cheese.

10 Using the oven gloves, place the baking tray under the grill for a few minutes. Watch it all the time in case the cheese burns.

11 When the cheese melts, bubbles and turns golden, use the oven gloves to remove the tray and set it on a heat-resistant surface.

12 Use the tongs or fish slice to lift – launch! – each torpedo on to a serving plate.

13 Serve hot. Dipping sticks of crunchy carrot into the melted cheese is a sensation not to be missed (see page 13)!

Be a Crafty Croc

To make this:

- **Dairy Free** – miss out the cheese and use humus.
- **Wheat** and **Gluten Free** – use special bread or rice cakes instead of bread.
- **Vegetarian** – mix pumpkin and sunflower seeds with the tomato instead of chicken.

Here are some other
mouth-watering ideas to try
on baguettes . . .

chopped **apple** sprinkled
with grated **cheese**

•

chopped, fried **bacon** with sliced
tomato, sprinkled with grated **cheese**

•

chopped up (cooked) **fish fingers**,
drizzled with **tomato ketchup** and
sprinkled with grated **cheese**

•

hot **baked beans** (or **spaghetti hoops**)
in tomato sauce, sprinkled with
grated **cheese**

•

grated **carrot** mixed with chopped **dates**
and sprinkled with grated **cheese**

•

tuna mixed with chopped **celery** and
sprinkled with grated **cheese**

•

diced (cooked) **chicken** mixed with
natural yoghurt and a little **curry
powder**, sprinkled with grated **cheese**

Snack Attack!

Sandwiches are all very well, but
sometimes you just feel like
something different. The next
recipes use all sorts of things to
hold lots of fillings. Why not try
out your own ideas too!

Snappy Socks!

Did you know that Crafty Croc has very tasty socks? You can make yours tasty too!

Wheat Free and **Gluten Free** pitta breads are now available – search for them in your local supermarket.

Have a Pitta Party – go to page 166 and use the Taco fillings to stuff your socks.

First, make your sock pocket to take your choice of yummy filling . . .

Serves 1

Takes 5 mins

No cooking

DB

DF

(GF)

V

VG

(WF)

You Will Need

1 pitta bread

sharp knife
chopping board

Snap To It!

1 Take a fresh pitta bread and carefully cut it in half across the middle.

2 Lift up a pitta half and you might be surprised to find that it is hollow inside – just ready for something good to fill it. This is your 'sock'! You can eat your sock cold, warmed a little in the toaster or oven, or heated for a few seconds in the microwave.

3 Gently squeeze the two edges together to pop the middle open to make a ready pocket for any filling you choose, sweet or savoury.

Be a Crafty Croc

'Now choose what you would like to fill your socks with – just turn the page to find out what I like to have in my socks . . .'

Cheesy socks!

This is Crafty Croc's Concoction – it doesn't go with a 'bang' like some experiments, but it might make your taste-buds explode!

Don't worry if you don't have all the ingredients listed at the end of the recipe, just use what you have. It's a mix and match sensation!

You Will Need

1 pitta bread – made into 2 'socks' (page 50)
125g tub cottage or cream cheese
(or humus)

Filling
Any or all of the ingredients listed opposite

bowl
wooden spoon
dessertspoon
chopping board
sharp knife
spatula
2 serving plates

Snap To It!

1 Use the sharp knife to chop your chosen fruit and vegetables on the chopping board (go to pages 10 to 15 to see how to do this).

2 Using the spatula, scrape out all the cottage or cream cheese into the bowl.

3 Add your chosen ingredients and mix well with the wooden spoon.

4 Use the dessertspoon to fill each 'sock' with the mixture.

5 Serve on two plates and enjoy all the different tastes and textures!

Be a Crafty Croc

If you have enjoyed your concoction, make a note of what you used so that you can enjoy it again. Experiment and have tasting sessions with your friends to choose the best.

Try any or all of the following . . .

• raisins •

• chopped celery •

• chopped crispy bacon •

• chopped spring onions •

• chopped apple •

• stone-less olives •

• chopped peppers •

• chopped pineapple •

• chopped tomatoes •

• tuna flakes •

• salted peanuts •

Has-bean Socks

Fill a warm pitta pocket with warm *baked beans* – sometimes Crafty Croc adds a few chunks of edam cheese to the beans. The cheese melts to make puddles of soft gooey cheese which pop up like surprises as you eat.

Make sure you are armed with a plate and plenty napkins or paper towels – 'Has-bean Socks' have a mind of their own. Adults tend to get rather steamed up when they don't land in your mouth!!

You Will Need

1 pitta bread – made into 2 'socks' (page 50)
1 small tin baked beans
50g (2oz) edam cheese

tin opener
bowl
dessertspoon
baking tray or microwave plate
oven gloves
fish slice
grater
2 plates to serve

Snap To It!

1 Use the roughest side of the grater to grate the cheese into the bowl. Be careful of your fingers, as the grater can be very sharp.

2 Pop about half the cheese into the pitta pocket.

3 Open the tin of baked beans with the tin opener, being careful of the sharp edges. Use the dessertspoon to scoop the beans into the two pittas.

4 Top with the rest of the cheese.

5 Lay the pittas on the baking tray or microwave plate and put on the oven gloves. Time to get cooking!

IN THE OVEN

a) Arrange the shelves in the oven so the baking tray can sit on the middle shelf. Turn on the oven to heat at Gas 4, 350°F or 180°C. Use the oven gloves to put the tray in the oven. Bake for 10 to 15 minutes.

b) Use the oven gloves to lift the tray from the oven and place it on a heat-resistant surface.

IN THE MICROWAVE

a) Put the 'socks' on to the microwave plate and cook on high for 30 seconds. Turn the plate and cook for another 20 seconds. Check to see if they are hot enough. If not, turn them and cook for another 20 seconds.

6 Use the fish slice to lift your Has-bean Socks on to the serving plates. Serve while still hot.

Be a Crafty Croc

- Add a little chilli powder to the beans to make a spicy dish.
- Of course, if you leave out the cheese, this becomes a **Dairy Free** or **Vegan** recipe.
- For non-vegetarians – chop up some cooked turkey, chicken, bacon or sausages and add it to the baked beans before you put them into the 'sock'.

Scrambled Socks

How many different textures can you find while you are eating 'Scrambled Socks'? I can think of at least three. What do you think they could be?

Serves 2

Takes 30 mins

Cook – hob
(or microwave)

DB

(GF)

VG

(WF)

You Will Need

1 pitta bread – made into 2 'socks' (page 50)
2 eggs
2 tbsp milk (semi-skimmed)
2 tbsp sweetcorn
1 tbsp tomato ketchup (low sugar)
pinch of salt

bowl
saucepan
wooden spoon
dessertspoon
tablespoon
oven gloves
2 serving plates
fish slice
teacup
fork

Be a Crafty Croc

Grated cheese, pieces of cooked ham or smoked salmon all make scrambled socks eggs-traspecially tasty!

Snap To It!

1 Crack the eggs one by one into the teacup and then into the bowl (see page 18).

2 Add the salt and milk to the eggs and beat with the fork.

3 Now to cook:

ON THE HOB

a) Pour the beaten eggs into the pan and put on the hob on a medium heat. Keep stirring all the time with the wooden spoon as the egg begins to set round the edges and bottom of the pan.

b) Gently, keep stirring the egg from the edges and bottom of the pan and mix it with the uncooked egg until it turns thick and creamy.

c) Turn off the heat and set the pan on a heat-resistant surface. If you cook the egg too much it will go very hard and rubbery with watery liquid and will not taste so good.

IN THE MICROWAVE

a) Put the bowl of egg mixture into the microwave and cook on high power for 1 minute. Stir and cook on high power for 20 second bursts (stirring each time the microwave stops) until the eggs are all thick and creamy.

b) Remove the bowl from the microwave using the oven gloves.

4 Stir the sweetcorn and tomato ketchup into the cooked eggs and leave to cool a little.

5 Use the dessertspoon to fill each 'sock' with the mixture.

6 Lift your 'socks' on to the plate with the fish slice and enjoy. (You can re-heat a little with a quick 20 second burst in the microwave or on a baking tray under a medium grill for a few minutes – remember to use oven gloves.)

Serves 2

Takes 5 mins

No cooking

DB

DF

(GF)

V

VG

(WF)

Bananas for Me

A bit messy to eat, but worth the bother!

You Will Need

1 pitta bread – made into 2 'socks' (page 50)
2 medium bananas
6 stoned dates

bowl
fork
kitchen scissors
tablespoon
2 soup bowls to serve

Snap To It!

1 Peel the bananas and put them in the bowl. Mash them to a creamy pulp using the fork.

2 Hold each date over the bowl and carefully use the scissors to cut them into small pieces so that they fall into the banana.

3 Mix in with the fork.

4 Spoon the mixture into the socks and then carefully lift each sock into the soup bowl.

5 Serve at once – a little messy but really worth it!

Amazingly Apple

Another way to stuff your socks!

Serves 2

Takes 5 mins

No cooking

DB

DF

(GF)

V

VG

(WF)

You Will Need

1 pitta bread – made into 2 'socks'
2 juicy apples – Cox's, Gala or Braeburn
4 apricots
handful of raisins
ground cinnamon

potato peeler
bowl
grater
kitchen scissors
dessertspoon
2 soup bowls to serve

Snap To It!

1 Peel and grate the apple into the bowl (see page 20).

2 Hold each apricot over the bowl and carefully use the scissors to cut them into small pieces.

3 Throw in the raisins. Sprinkle with a pinch of cinnamon and stir well with the spoon.

4 Spoon the mixture into the two socks.

5 Serve in the soup bowls and get your teeth into something a bit different!

Snappy Snaps

Serves 2

Takes 10 mins

No cooking

DB

GF

VG

WF

Sometimes we need something crisp to eat instead of soft bread. Crocodiles also like crunchy food – and make it snappy!

You Will Need

4 rice cakes
cream cheese (try low fat)
cucumber
2 spring onions
1 carrot
1 apple
1 tomato
French dressing (low fat)

chopping board
sharp knife
knife for spreading
scissors
grater
bowl
potato peeler
teaspoon
tablespoon
plate

Be a Crafty Croc

Try cottage cheese instead of cream cheese. Try a tasty mixture of chopped pineapple, sweetcorn and red and green peppers instead of carrot, apple and spring onion.

Snap To It!

1 Wash and dry the cucumber. Place it on the chopping board and, being careful, use the sharp knife to chop off 4 thin slices.

2 Wash, dry and slice the tomato (see page 15).

3 Wash and peel the carrot with the potato peeler. Use the roughest part of the grater to carefully grate it into the bowl.

4 Wash the apple and carefully grate it into the bowl too.

5 Wash the spring onions and use the scissors to cut off the stringy roots and about 2cm (1 inch) from the tops. Cut the spring onions into the bowl with the carrot and apple. (Try to cut them as small as you can, but be careful not to cut your fingers!)

6 Add a teaspoon of dressing and mix everything well together with the tablespoon.

7 Spread cheese on one side of each of the rice cakes and add a spoonful of the carrot mixture.

8 Place a slice of tomato on top, then place a slice of cucumber on top of the tomato, so that it is just overlapping it.

9 Do the same with the other snaps.

10 Serve on the plate at once (they do go a bit soggy if left)!

Be a Crafty Croc

Try other snaps like **Oatcakes** – top with:
• thin slices of smoked barbecue ham, slices of cucumber and chopped pineapple.
• flaked tuna, chopped red pepper and grated apple.
• sliced banana and chopped, crisp smoky bacon.

Cream crackers – spread with:
• mustard, a slice of cheese and a slice of tomato.
• cream cheese with chopped chives sprinkled on top.
YUM!

Surprise
Melted Cheese Crunch

Serves 2

Takes 10 mins

Cook – grill

DB

(GF)

VG

(WF)

A quick snack for a cold day – make nibbly ones using smaller biscuits for a party snack which will be snapped up!

You Will Need

4 large biscuits
(oatcakes or digestives or rich teas)
110g (4oz) cheddar cheese (low fat)
Worcester sauce or tomato ketchup

baking tray
oven gloves
fish slice
chopping board
sharp knife
knife for spreading
plate

Snap To It!

1 Carefully, use the sharp knife to chop the cheese into thin slices on the chopping board.

2 Take two of the biscuits and cover with some of the cheese slices.

3 Drizzle with a few drops of Worcester sauce.

4 Spread the other two biscuits with tomato ketchup. Then cover them with the rest of the cheese slices.

5 Put all four biscuits on to the baking tray.

6 Heat the grill to medium.

7 Put on the oven gloves and carefully place the baking tray under the grill. Watch the biscuits all the time. As soon as the cheese has melted, use the oven gloves to lift out the tray and set it on a heat-resistant surface.

8 Use the fish slice to place the cheesy biscuits on to a serving plate. Serve hot with a dish of sweet cherry tomatoes, if you have them.

Be a Crafty Croc

Wheat Free – use wheat-free oatcakes to make this recipe.

Basmati Rice

Serves 4

Takes 30 mins

Cook – hob

DB

DF

GF

V

VG

WF

There are many different varieties of rice used in cooking. Basmati is Crafty Croc's favourite – when he smells the special aroma it reminds him of hot countries and of home!

Go to page 53 to find ideas for tasty things you can stir into your cooked rice. Make your own concoction!

You Will Need

2 breakfast cups of basmati rice
1 tsp salt
water

deep saucepan
pyrex dish + lid
large bowl
sieve
teaspoon
oven gloves

Snap To It!

1 Put the rice and salt into a deep saucepan and cover well with cold water.

2 Place the pan on the hob and turn the heat to high. Bring to the boil, then turn down the heat so that the water is just moving in the pan but not boiling over.

3 Cook for 12 minutes – make sure that the water in the pan does not dry up by adding more hot water if you need to.

4 After 12 minutes, dip a teaspoon into the water to lift out some rice. When it has cooled, taste the rice to see that it is soft.

5 Turn on the cold water tap. Place the sieve in the bowl and set them in the sink.

6 Carefully, lift the pan off the heat and pour the rice through the sieve. Then hold the sieve under the cold running water for a few minutes – this will wash away the sticky starch from the rice and leave the grains separated.

7 Set the sieve over the pan for a few minutes to drain out the water. Then tip the rice into the pyrex dish and put on the lid.

Be a Clever Croc

Cooked rice should be kept in the fridge for only one day.

To re-heat your rice

IN THE MICROWAVE

Put the pyrex dish in the microwave and heat on high for 2 minutes, stirring halfway through. Use oven gloves to lift out the dish when it is ready.

IN THE OVEN

Heat the oven to Gas 4, 350°F or 180°C. Use oven gloves to put the pyrex dish in the oven. Cook for 15 to 20 minutes. Remember to use oven gloves to lift the dish out of the oven and set it on a heat-resistant surface.

Make it a Melt

This recipe uses leftovers to make a quick and easy snack. If you don't have leftovers you can cook the ingredients. It takes longer, but it's worth it! Or try sweetcorn and chopped peppers instead of beans, or flaked tuna instead of chicken or ham. Add nuts, raisins and sultanas, chopped apple or banana for extra textures.

Add what you like to make it your own personal melt – remember to write down the recipe or you may forget it. See page 53 for some ideas to start you off.

You Will Need

150g (6oz) cooked rice (see page 64)
1 small tin baked beans
110g (4oz) cooked ham, chicken
(or any other cooked meat)
50g (2oz) mushrooms, chopped, cooked
50g (2oz) onions, chopped, cooked
110g (4oz) edam cheese
chilli or Worcester sauce (if you like)

deep oven-proof dish + lid
bowl
tin opener
grater
wooden spoon
oven gloves
plate

Snap To It!

1 Cook the rice (you'll find the recipe on the previous page).

2 Use the roughest side of the grater to grate the cheese on to the plate. Be careful of your fingers, as the grater can be very sharp.

3 Add the rice and all the other ingredients – except the cheese – to the bowl and mix together. You can add a touch of chilli or Worcester sauce if you like spicy food.

4 Put the mixture into an oven-proof dish and put on the lid. Cook:

IN THE MICROWAVE

Place the dish in the microwave and cook for 1 minute on high. Stir and microwave for another minute on high.

IN THE OVEN

a) Arrange the oven shelves so the dish can sit on the middle shelf. Turn on the oven to heat at Gas 6, 400°F or 200°C.

b) Use oven gloves to place the dish in the hot oven. Bake for 20 minutes.

5 Using oven gloves, lift the dish out of the microwave or oven and set on a heat-resistant surface. Still wearing oven gloves, carefully remove the lid.

6 Turn on the grill to heat at medium.

7 Sprinkle the grated cheese over the rice mixture and put your oven gloves back on to put the dish under the heated grill. Melt the cheese until it bubbles and turns golden.

8 Use oven gloves to lift the dish from under the grill and set it on a heat-resistant surface.

9 Serve on the plate at once! Carrot sticks (see page 13) are great dipped into the cheesy topping.

Be a Crafty Croc

To make this a **Dairy Free** melt, use non-dairy cheese or just leave the cheese out and call it a '*Splodge*' instead!

Loch Ness Monster

Crafty Croc is great friends with Scotland's famous but shy monster. When the two get together, this is one of their favourite snacks.

You Will Need

1 long crusty baguette
50g (2oz) sunflower spread (dairy free)
1 packet cheese slices
tomato ketchup
2 cherry tomatoes
cucumber

aluminium foil
baking tray
sharp knife
chopping board
knife for spreading
bread knife
plate
2 wooden cocktail sticks
oven gloves

Be a Crafty Croc

Gluten Free and **Wheat Free** – be adventurous and use mini rice cakes instead of the baguette. (Watch they do not burn in the oven.) A crisp and gooey sensation! Try other fillings instead of cheese to make this a **Dairy Free** monster – sliced ham or bacon or flaked tuna and tomato taste delicious!

Snap To It !

1 Arrange the shelves in the oven so the baking tray can sit on the middle shelf. Turn on the oven to heat at Gas 6, 400°F or 200°C.

2 Cut a piece of foil large enough to wrap the baguette in, leaving plenty of room all around.

3 Place the cheese slices on the chopping board and cut them in half. Place the pieces on a plate.

4 Place the baguette on the chopping board and cut it into thick slices using the bread knife.

5 Keeping the slices in order so that you can stick the baguette together again, spread each slice with margarine and then with tomato ketchup.

6 Place a half slice of cheese on top of the tomato ketchup and sandwich the next piece of baguette on to it.

7 Gradually put the loaf back together again by adding the next slice of baguette on to the cheese.

8 Wrap the loaf in aluminium foil.

9 Place the parcel on the baking tray and use oven gloves to put the tray in the oven. Bake for about 10 to 15 minutes.

10 Using oven gloves, remove the tray from the oven and set it on a heat-resistant surface. Leave to cool for a couple of minutes.

11 Carefully open the foil away from your face so that the escaping hot steam doesn't burn you.

12 Pop a cherry tomato on to the end of each cocktail stick.

13 Place the cucumber on the chopping board and use the sharp knife to slice it in two.

14 Decide which end of the loaf looks more like a face and then insert the tomatoes on sticks to make the eyes. Use the bread knife to make a slit where the mouth should be and stick in the half slice of cucumber. Trim the other half slice of cucumber to make a nose and use ketchup to stick it on.

15 Serve the beastie in the foil on the tray.

All Day Breakfast

Serves 2

Takes 10 mins

Cook – hob
(or microwave)

DB

DF

(GF)

V

VG

WF

This is a tasty, healthy way to start the day. Since you can eat this 'breakfast' almost anywhere, there's no need to keep it just for the morning. Take it on a picnic, to school as part of a packed lunch, or even eat it for your supper!

Be adventurous with the dried fruit – choose from:

• raisins •
• sultanas •
• cranberries •
• chopped apricots •

You Will Need

110g (4oz) rolled oats (millet or quinoa)
50g (2oz) dried fruit
(raisins, sultanas, cranberries . . . you choose)
1 tbsp sunflower oil

deep pan
wooden spoon
tablespoon
bowl

Snap To It !

1 Mix the fruit and oats in the bowl.

2 Pour the oil into the pan and then put the pan on the hob. Turn the heat to medium.

3 Add the oats and fruit mixture, turn the heat to low and stir everything together using the wooden spoon.

4 Keep stirring for about 2 minutes so that everything is heated.

5 All Day Breakfast can be served hot or cold, with milk, yoghurt, apple juice or water. Crafty Croc has lots of great ideas!

Be a Crafty Croc

This makes a very tasty pudding! Serve it hot or cold –
* stirred into creamy custard
* sprinkled over ice cream, rice pudding, strawberries, stewed apples or rhubarb
* as a hot 'mushy' dish . . .

To Make Hot Mushy All Day Breakfast

IN THE MICROWAVE

a) Mix half a cup of the All Day Breakfast in a bowl with one cup of milk, apple juice or water. Stir well.

b) Put the bowl in the microwave and cook for 2 minutes on high.

c) Stir and then cook another minute. Leave to stand for 1 minute and then carefully pour the mixture into a dish and serve.

ON THE HOB

a) Mix half a cup of the All Day Breakfast in a saucepan with one cup of milk, apple juice or water. Stir well.

b) Put the saucepan on the hob and turn the heat to medium.

c) Cook for 2 minutes, stirring all the time until thick and creamy.

d) Lift the pan off the hob and set on a heat-resistant surface to cool. Then carefully pour the mixture into a dish and serve.

Tarka Dhal

This is a kind of curry, traditionally served with bread or rice (there's a recipe for rice on page 64), but you can also use it as a filling for pittas (see page 50). Messy but tasty! Or use it as a dip for sticks of carrot or celery or Vegetable Traffic Lights (see page 152). You can also serve it as a topping on toast or baked potatoes. You decide!

Serves 4

Takes 1 hour

Cook – hob

DB

DF

GF

V

VG

WF

You Will Need

2 large onions
230g (8oz) split red lentils
0.5 litres (⅝ pint) water
1½ tsp tumeric
1 tbsp ground cumin
90g (3½oz) vegetable ghee (or margarine)
1 tbsp garlic puree (or crushed garlic)
1 small tin (125g) chopped tomatoes
½ tsp crushed dried chillies
(or 1 level tsp chilli powder)
1 tbsp chopped fresh coriander
(or 1 tsp ground coriander)
1 tsp salt

tin opener
sharp knife
chopping board
bowl
sieve
2 saucepans
wooden spoon
teaspoon
tablespoon
garlic press
saucer

Snap To It!

1 Put the lentils into a sieve and hold under running water to wash them. Drain off the water through the sieve.

2 Put the lentils in a bowl, cover with fresh cold water and leave to soak for 30 minutes.

3 Peel the onions, place them on the chopping board and chop with the sharp knife (see page 14).

4 Pull 2 garlic cloves off the main bulb of garlic. Peel the cloves and push them through the garlic press on to a saucer.

5 Put the soaked lentils into a saucepan and pour in 0.5 litres of fresh water.

6 Add the tumeric and cumin and place the pan on the hob.

7 Turn on the heat and bring the water to the boil. Boil for 3 minutes. Then turn the heat to low so that the water is just moving in the pan. This is called simmering. Stir in half a teaspoon of salt and cook for 2 minutes.

8 Put the ghee in the other saucepan. Place it on the hob and turn the heat to medium to melt the ghee.

9 Add the garlic and fry the mixture for a minute.

10 Add the chopped onion and the dried chillies. Keep stirring with the wooden spoon until the onions turn soft but not brown.

11 Open the tin of tomatoes and add them to the onion mixture.

12 Stir in the coriander and bring to the boil.

13 Add half a teaspoon of salt and stir well.

14 Very carefully add the cooked lentils (there should be very little water left in the lentils). Stir the mixture well with the wooden spoon, turn off the heat and serve.

Be a Clever Croc

Keep your Dhal well covered in the fridge and it will keep for up to 3 days. It tastes great hot or cold!

Stovies

Serves 4

Takes 1 hour 30 mins

Cook – hob

DB

DF

(GF)

(VG)

(WF)

In one national survey to find the most popular food – mashed potatoes and stovies came out tops! Try this healthy version. It is a great dish to make round a camp fire.

You can even make your own oatcakes to go with the Stovies. The recipe is on the next page.

You Will Need

225g (8oz) cooked chopped turkey (or chicken)
675g (1½lb) potatoes
2 large onions
2 tbsp light olive oil
1 tsp sea salt
4 oatcakes

strong, deep pan with lid
bowl
wooden spoon
chopping board
sharp knife
teaspoon
potato peeler
tablespoon
4 soup plates

Snap To It!

1 Peel the potatoes under cold running water.

2 Place one potato on the chopping board and carefully use the sharp knife to cut it in half. Take one half, place the flat side down on the board and carefully cut the potato into slices.

3 Do the same with all the potatoes. Put the slices into the bowl.

4 Peel the onions and place one on the chopping board. Carefully use the sharp knife to cut it in half. Take one half, place the flat side down on the board and carefully cut the onion into slices.

5 Do the same with the other onion.

6 Add the oil to the pan and place the pan on the hob. Turn the heat to medium.

7 Add the sliced onions and cook over a medium heat, stirring with the wooden spoon until they are soft and golden.

8 Turn the heat to low and add the sliced potatoes to the pan.

9 Add the salt and stir with the wooden spoon.

10 Put the lid on the pan and cook over a very low heat, stirring every 10 minutes to make sure that nothing sticks to the pan. Cook for 30 minutes or until the potatoes are soft and breaking.

11 Stir in the cooked chicken or turkey. Cook for another 5 minutes to make sure everything is heated through.

12 Serve piled into the deep soup plates with an oatcake stuck on the top.

Be a Crafty Croc

Wheat Free diets – make sure that there is no wheat flour in the oatcakes you buy.

Gluten Free diets – if you can't eat oatmeal, have rice cakes instead!!

Vegetarians can miss out the turkey or chicken and stir in grated cheese or cooked lentils instead.

Oatcakes

Makes 8
oatcakes

Takes 30 mins

Cook – oven

DB

DF

V

VG

WF

Oatmeal was very important in Scotland. It was used as a food, as a face-wash, to preserve meat and cheese, and even instead of money! It can really be called the first fast-food snack!

Oatcakes taste best when they are lightly toasted and the time this takes depends on the oatmeal you use and the amount of water needed to mix your oatcake. They burn easily so you need to watch them carefully as they bake.

You Will Need

110g (4oz) fine or medium oatmeal
5ml sunflower oil (or olive oil)
pinch of sea salt
warm water to mix
fine oatmeal to roll out

rolling pin
scales
bowl
wooden spoon
baking tray
oven gloves
teaspoon
tablespoon
palette knife
wire cooling rack

Snap To It!

1. Arrange the shelves in the oven so the baking tray can sit on the top shelf. Turn on the oven to heat at Gas 5, 375°F or 190°C.

2. Measure the oatmeal into the bowl – use scales if you have them, otherwise 4 tablespoons of oatmeal is about right.

3. Add the salt and oil. Then mix in some water a little at at time and stir with the wooden spoon to make a dough which forms a smooth, softish lump and leaves the sides of the bowl clean.

4. Shake a little oatmeal on to a clean work surface and then put the lump of dough on to it. Shake a little oatmeal on top – this stops the rolling pin sticking to the dough.

5. Roll out the dough, trying to keep a round shape, until it is thin like an oatcake or biscuit. Turn the dough each time you give it a roll out so that you are not rolling it in the same direction all the time. If the dough sticks to the work surface or rolling pin use the palette knife to loosen it and then shake a little more oatmeal on to the work surface and rolling pin.

6. Carefully use the knife to cut the round flat oatcake into 8 even triangles, called 'farls'. Lift them on to the baking tray.

7. Using the oven gloves, lift the tray into the oven and cook till dry and crisp – this will take 12 to 15 minutes. Watch carefully because oatmeal burns easily.

8. Use the oven gloves to take the tray out of the oven and set it on a heat-resistant surface.

9. Use the palette knife to lift the oatcakes on to the wire cooling rack to cool completely.

10. Serve cold with any sweet or savoury spread you like.

Be a Crafty Croc

Keep practicing! You can make all sorts of shapes.
Oatcakes are very good to eat alone as a snack and with cheese, dips, jam and honey.

Hot Noodle

Use your noodle! That's all you really need for this – anything else you want to add is up to you.

Pack this into a tub and eat it cold as a delicious salad snack instead of sandwiches – YUM!

You Will Need

225g (8oz) rice noodles (thin)

1 small tin sweetcorn – drained
50g (2oz) cooked garden peas
1 carrot – peeled and chopped
2 spring onions – chopped
110g (4oz) cooked chicken meat – chopped
50g (2oz) cooked chopped ham (or pepperami)
1 dessertspoon tomato ketchup
1 dash Worcestershire sauce (if you like)
1 tsp salt

deep, heat-proof bowl
oven or microwave dish + lid
wooden spoon
tin opener
sharp knife
chopping board
sieve
dessertspoon
teaspoon
bowl
oven gloves
serving bowl
chopsticks

Snap To It!

1 Put the rice noodles into a deep, heat-proof bowl and then carefully pour in enough boiling water to cover them.

2 Add 1 teaspoon of salt and leave to soak for 5 minutes.

3 Hold a sieve over the sink and pour the noodles into the sieve to drain. Rinse them in cold running water for a few minutes to cool.

4 Place the sieve on top of the bowl and let the noodles drain well. Then tip the noodles into an oven or microwave-proof dish (depending on how you are going to cook your noodles).

5 Add all the other ingredients and stir well with the wooden spoon. Now choose how you are going to cook it.

IN THE MICROWAVE

a) Put the lid on the dish and place in the microwave. Cook on high power for 1 minute.

b) Stir and check the noodles are hot. If not, cook for another minute and check again. Cook, stir and check until the noodles are hot.

IN THE OVEN

a) Heat your oven to Gas 6, 400°F or 200°C.

b) Put the lid on the dish and use the oven gloves to carefully place it in the oven. Cook for 20 minutes until hot.

6 Use the oven gloves to lift the dish from the oven or microwave and place on a heat-resistant surface.

7 Serve in a bowl with chopsticks, if you have them, and eat at once.

Be a Crafty Croc

You can add what you like to the noodles – try prawns, courgettes, peppers, onions, spicy curry sauce or sweet and sour sauce.

• **Vegans** and **Vegetarians** – miss out the meat.

Crepes

Serves 4

Takes 30 mins

Cook – hob

DB

DF

(GF)

(VG)

(WF)

These are lovely thin pancakes which you can eat as a savoury or sweet snack. They are great for making wraps – try the recipe on the next page.

You can also fill them like pitta bread (*see* pages 52 to 59). A lovely sweet banana and chocolate filling is on page 130, or simply eat your crepes just as they are – drizzle them with some lemon juice and sugar while just warm, roll up and eat at once!

You Will Need

225g (8oz) plain flour (or buckwheat flour)
1 large egg
300ml (½ pint) liquid
(for savoury crepes use water, chicken stock or milk)
(for sweet crepes use water, milk or apple juice)
1 tsp cooking oil (sunflower or light olive oil)
pinch of salt
lemon juice
a little sugar

large bowl
sieve
non-stick heavy frying pan
wooden spoon or wire balloon whisk
fish slice or palette knife
ladle
wire tray
clean tea towel
kitchen towel
teaspoon

Snap To It!

1 Put the sieve over the bowl and shake the flour through it – this is called 'sifting'– there are two reasons for doing this. One: to catch any foreign bodies and lumps! Two: to add more air into the mixture.

2 Add the egg and the salt. Beat the liquid with the wooden spoon or whisk until you have a smooth mixture (called a batter) like thick single cream.

3 Stir in 1 teaspoon of oil and leave the mixture to rest for a few minutes.

4 Fold the tea towel in two and set it on the wire tray. Place the wire tray beside the hob.

5 Rub the pan with a little oil using the kitchen towel. Place the pan on the hob and heat for a few minutes at medium.

6 Carefully, pour a ladle of batter into the hot pan and swirl the pan around to cover the bottom with a thin coating of batter.

7 After about 1 or 2 minutes, bubbles will appear on top of the batter. Use the fish slice or palette knife to lift up the crepe and flip it over to cook the other side. Cook for another minute.

8 Open the tea towel envelope, set the pancake inside and cover with the tea towel. Your pancake will stay warm and soft while you make the remaining crepes.

9 Repeat with the rest of the batter.

10 Serve. If you want to eat them just as they are, drizzle each one with lemon juice, sprinkle on a little sugar and roll the crepe up.

Be a Crafty Croc

You can freeze crepes: leave out the lemon juice and sugar, and freeze flat, individually wrapped in cling film in a labelled poly bag.

Crepes can be stuffed with lots of things - sweet or savoury - have fun experimenting with your own ideas!

That's a Wrap!

Serves 2

Takes 30 mins

Cook – grill

DB

(DF)

(GF)

(V)

(VG)

(WF)

This is a lovely hot recipe for a cold day and a real favourite of Croc's.

You can buy ready-made wraps – plain and flavoured (Gluten or Wheat Free) – in most supermarkets now. If you don't have wraps, you can make the crepes on the previous page and fill them instead.

You Will Need

2 ready-made wraps
110g (4oz) cheddar cheese
1 heaped tsp flour
2 tbsp milk
shake of Worcestershire sauce – if you like spicy food

bowl
grater
wooden spoon
spreading knife
2 flat serving plates
baking tray
tablespoon
oven gloves
fish slice
teaspoon
knife
fork

Snap To It!

1 Turn on the grill to heat at medium.

2 Use the roughest side of the grater to grate the cheese into the bowl. Be careful of your fingers, as the grater can be very sharp.

3 Add the flour, milk and sauce to the cheese. Mix to a paste using the wooden spoon.

4 Lay the two wraps flat on the baking tray and divide the cheese paste between them.

5 Spread the mixture out to the edges, using the knife.

6 Using the oven gloves, put the tray under the hot grill. Watch carefully. Cook for about 3 minutes until golden and bubbling.

7 Use the oven gloves to take the tray out from the grill and place it on a heat-resistant surface.

8 Use the fish slice to lift each wrap on to a plate.

9 Now for the tricky bit. Using a knife and fork (remember the wrap is hot!) quickly roll each wrap up into a torpedo shape.

10 Serve warm with a handful of sweet cherry tomatoes if you have them.

Be a Crafty Croc

- **Dairy Free** – try a tuna and tomato filling instead of cheese, or fill your wrap with *bolognaise* sauce (you can buy this ready made).
- **Vegan** – use humus instead of cheese.

Be adventurous! There are lots of ready-made healthy sauces and fillings in the chill cabinet at your local store.
Go to page 90 for other ideas.

Buckwheat Blaster

Easy to make and tasty to eat!

Great for **Gluten Free** and **Wheat Free** diets, as well as **diabetics**, and you can make this recipe **Dairy Free** too by using soya milk and soya cheese.

You Will Need

150g (6oz) buckwheat flour
1 large egg (or 2 small eggs)
1 tsp gluten-free baking powder
(or ½ teaspoon bicarbonate of soda)
1 tsp cream of tartare
pinch of salt
milk to mix – about 300ml
sunflower oil

Topping
cream cheese (low fat)

bowl
sieve
balloon whisk or wooden spoon
palette knife or fish slice
wire cooling tray
2 clean tea towels
tablespoon
teaspoon
knife for spreading
oven gloves
large frying pan or girdle

Snap To It !

1   Organise your equipment before you start to cook – lay 2 clean tea towels flat on a wire cooling tray beside the cooker. When you make your pancakes you will put each one between the tea towels to keep them warm.

2   Sieve the buckwheat flour into a bowl.

3   Add the bicarbonate of soda (or baking powder), cream of tartare and salt. Mix well.

4   Make a well in the middle of the flour and add the eggs one at a time (see page 18).

5   Using a balloon whisk or wooden spoon beat in enough milk to make a smooth batter which is like thick double cream.

6   Rub the girdle or frying pan with a little oil and then place it on the hob and turn on the heat. Drop a little batter on to the pan to see if it is hot enough. Bubbles should appear on the surface and, when you flip it over with the palette knife, the cooked side will be a dark golden colour. You are ready to cook the rest of your pancakes.

7   Use the tablespoon to carefully pour a spoonful of batter on to the pan. Turn the pancake over when bubbles appear on the top.

8   Carefully ease the palette knife under the pancake. Lift and flip it over to cook the other side. Cook it for about 1 minute. Then lift your pancake on to the cooling tray and wrap in the towel.

9   Repeat until all the batter is used up.

10 Now for the best bit – topping! Put your Buckwheat Blaster pancake on a plate, spread it with cream cheese and serve.

Be a Crafty Croc

Why stop at cheese! Sprinkle on prawns, or little pieces of pineapple, or ham, or even spiced pepperami for a hot treat! See page 90 for other ideas!

Splendid Little Spuds

Little baby boiling potatoes are very versatile and easy to prepare. You can also buy pre-boiled potatoes in most supermarkets, which makes this recipe even easier to make!

If you like this recipe, you will have to try Christmas Dinner Jackets (page 172).

Serves 4

Takes 1 hour

Cook – grill

DB

DF

GF

(V)

(VG)

WF

You Will Need

1 large tin (or packet) of baby potatoes
1 large packet of smoked bacon rashers
(or quorn rashers)
1 level tsp salt

deep saucepan
tin opener
colander or sieve
large plate
wooden skewers
food tongs
baking tray
oven gloves

Snap To It!

1 Open the tin or packet of cooked baby potatoes or cook them:

 a) Wash the potatoes and put them in the deep saucepan.

 b) Add the salt and place the pan on the hob. Turn the heat to high. Bring to the boil and put the lid on the pan.

 c) Turn the heat to low. Cook for 10 to 20 minutes until tender.

2 Drain the potatoes in a colander in the sink. (Leave hot potatoes to cool until you can handle them.)

3 Put the potatoes on to the large plate.

4 Wrap a rasher of lean smoked bacon round each potato.

5 Carefully, spear two potatoes on to each of the small wooden skewers and place these on to a baking tray.

6 Wearing oven gloves, carefully place the baking tray under a medium grill.

7 After 5 minutes, carefully use the oven gloves to lift out the tray and set it on a heat-resistant surface.

8 Use the tongs to turn the potatoes and place the tray back under the grill.

9 Keep turning and grilling until the bacon is crisp and the potatoes are heated through. Be careful of the hot grill and wear oven gloves all the time.

10 Carefully, use the oven gloves to lift out the tray and set it on a heat-resistant surface.

11 Use the tongs to lift the potatoes on to your plate and serve.

Be a Crafty Croc

Try spreading the bacon with honey mustard (or ordinary mustard) or chutney.

You can make this recipe for a barbecue – prepare the potatoes earlier in the day and keep in the fridge, ready to pop on the barbecue when you need them.

Baked Jacket Potatoes

Serves 1

Takes 15 mins
(or 1 hour 10
mins in oven)

Cook – oven
(or microwave)

DB

(DF)

GF

(V)

VG

WF

The best potatoes to use for baking are those which are dry and floury inside – like Cara, Pentland Squire, Maris Piper, Cultura, Record. Most pre-packed potatoes tell you on the bag if they are good for baking. Some new potatoes are good to bake too – try Cyprus and Egyptian.

While your potato is cooking, think about what you want inside it. You can just have it topped with butter or go to page 90 for some more interesting ideas.

You Will Need

a medium to large evenly shaped potato
butter (or dairy free spread)

kitchen towel
skewer or sharp knife
plate (microwave) or baking tray (oven)
fork
plate or soup bowl
oven gloves

Snap To It!

1 Scrub your potato really well in cold running water.

2 Prick it all over with a fork – this is to prevent the skin exploding!

3 Now to cook. There are two ways to bake your potato:

IN THE MICROWAVE

If you have a microwave potato baker, push the spike into the potato. It will conduct heat into the middle and cut down the time of cooking. Follow the instructions. If you don't have a baker –

a) Put a sheet of kitchen towel on the microwave plate, lay the potato on it and cook on full power for 4 minutes.

b) Using oven gloves, turn the potato over and cook on full power for another 4 minutes.

c) Test with a skewer or the point of a knife to make sure that the potato is tender all the way through. If it is not cooked you will feel a hard bit in the middle. Cook for 1 minute and then test again. Keep cooking and testing until the potato is cooked.

IN THE OVEN

a) Arrange the shelves in the oven so that the baking tray can sit on the middle shelf. Heat the oven to Gas 6, 400°F or 200°C.

b) If you have a metal skewer, carefully push this through the middle of your potato. It will conduct heat into the middle and cut down the time of cooking.

c) Set the potato on the baking tray and use oven gloves to put the tray in the hot oven. Bake for 1 hour.

d) Use the oven gloves to lift the tray out and set it on a heat-resistant surface. Test the potato with a skewer or the point of a knife to make sure that it is tender all the way through. If it is not cooked you will feel a hard bit in the middle. If it is not ready, bake for another 15 minutes. Use oven gloves!

e) Test the potato again. If it is still hard, bake for another 15 minutes. It should be ready by then!

4 Wear oven gloves to lift your cooked potato on to a plate, or try putting it into a soup bowl instead – the filling stays in!

fillings + spreads

DB

DF

GF

V

VG

WF

Veggies Choice

Humus or **tahini** makes a great filling for pancakes, wraps, pittas, baked potatoes, tacos or even just spread on bread.

Humus is a smooth creamy spread made from chick peas. **Tahini** is a tasty creamy spread made from ground sesame seeds, so you should not eat it if you have a nut allergy.

Pop your pancake, wrap, pitta bread, potato or taco on to a plate and use a knife to spread or fill with humus or tahini. Add lovely crisp shredded **lettuce**, sliced **tomatoes** or sliced **cucumber** for something different.

Be a Crafty Croc

Try sprinkling some spiced **crispy noodles** or **Bombay mix** (really spicy) on your humus or tahini (<u>not</u> for **Gluten** or **Wheat Free** diets).

Guacamole For All

This is made with **avocados**. See page 12 for how to prepare an avocado. Scoop out the flesh with a teaspoon and put it into a bowl. Add some **lemon juice** and mash with a fork. Mix in a pinch of **chilli powder** and one chopped **spring onion**.

Pop your pancake, wrap, pitta bread or potato on to a plate, heap the avocado mixture on top and tuck in. Looks and tastes F.A.B.! Guacamole also makes a great dip for tacos (see page 166).

DB

DF

GF

V

VG

WF

Tuna Drifter

small tin of tuna fish – drained
2 tbsp sweetcorn – drained
2 tsp mayonnaise (low fat)
pinch of chilli powder
red pepper – chopped

WF

DB

Mix everything together in a bowl and pile on to baked potatoes, stuff into tacos, pitta bread or spread in sandwiches.

Cheesed On

Cream cheese tastes delicious! Try it on pancakes, in wraps, pittas, tacos or on baked potatoes with pineapple, prawns, smoked ham, sliced tomatoes or spiced pepperami for those who like it hot!

DB

GF

(VG)

WF

91

Fast and easy fillings

Choose one (or more!) of these fillings for a tasty treat. Since they come in packets, tins, jars or tubs, all you need to do is open them and stuff your pancake, wrap, pitta bread, potato or taco. Yum!

baked beans (warm or cold)

a gooey slice of **Brie** or grated cheddar cheese

humus and **sweetcorn**

cottage cheese
(or grated low-fat cheese) with chopped **ham**

cream cheese and crispy **bacon**

a dollop of creamy **coleslaw**

ready-made **bolognaise sauce**

tuna and **sweetcorn**

sardines in tomato sauce

crisp shredded **lettuce** with chopped **peppers** and **tuna**

Sweet Selection

For a quick sweet snack just fill with any of the following –

mashed **banana**

grated **apple** and **raisins** mixed together

scoops of your favourite **ice cream**

chocolate spread

sliced **strawberries** and **cream**

Thirst Quenchers

After all those snacks, you must be ready for a drink! Here are some juices which will refresh any parched croc!

Smoothies

Be adventurous – try one of the most delicious drinks to come from America. Once you get the hang of how to make them, you can make up your own recipes. Use frozen fruit if you can – it makes your smoothie much thicker and creamier.

Get Freezing !

The day before you want to make your smoothie (or at least a few hours in advance) prepare and freeze the fruit.

Fruits to try are . . .

- apples -
- bananas -
- nectarines -
- peaches -
- strawberries -

Frozen bananas are useful in all smoothies – they make the drink thick and creamy, and they are easy to prepare. Just peel your banana, cut it into chunks and freeze on a flat tray until the pieces are firm. Then put them in a container – remember to label it (write the date on as well) – and pop them in the freezer for up to 6 months (see page 146).

Be a Clever Croc

'Once you have some containers of frozen fruit in the deep freeze, it is easy to make a smoothie any time.'

Very Berry Blitz

This is very berry good!

You Will Need

12 large strawberries
425ml (¾ pint) fresh apple juice
6 chunks of frozen banana
1 tbsp ice

blender or liquidiser
2 large glasses
2 straws
tablespoon
tea towel

Snap To It!

1 Put all the ingredients into the blender (or liquidiser). Put on the lid – even old crocs forget to do this so make sure you place it on firmly. Put a tea towel over the lid to help you hold the blender steady while you switch it on. Be prepared in case the blender jumps a bit – this is caused by the frozen fruit and ice in the mixture.

2 Blend on slow to begin with and gradually increase the speed until the mixture is smooth and creamy.

3 Pour into the two glasses, drop a straw into each and enjoy.

Honey Fruit Smoothie

Bored with breakfast? In need of a quick energy and vitamin fix?

Honey Fruit Smoothie is the answer!

You Will Need

300ml (½ pint) milk (low fat)
1 tbsp runny honey
1 tbsp wheatgerm
1 tbsp frozen, chopped banana
1 tbsp apple, chopped
1 tbsp thick and creamy yoghurt
1 tbsp crushed ice

Topping
ground cinnamon or drinking chocolate

blender or liquidiser
sharp knife
bowl
chopping board
potato peeler
tablespoon
tea towel
2 tall glasses
2 straws

Snap To It!

1 Using the potato peeler, peel the apple. Place it on the chopping board and carefully cut it into four pieces using the sharp knife.

2 Carefully cut out the core from one quarter and chop this quarter into small squares about 1cm. (Place the other quarters in a bowl and cover with cold water. Add a little lemon juice to prevent the fruit turning brown. You can eat these later.)

3 Put all the ingredients – except the ground cinnamon or drinking chocolate – into the blender (or liquidiser).

4 Put on the lid – even old crocs forget to do this so make sure you place it on firmly. Put a tea towel over the lid to help you hold the blender steady while you switch it on. Be prepared in case the blender jumps a bit – this is caused by the frozen fruit and ice in the mixture.

5 Blend on slow to begin with and gradually increase the speed until the mixture is smooth and creamy.

6 Pour into the two glasses and pop a straw into each glass.

7 Serve with a sprinkling of ground cinnamon or drinking chocolate on top.

Be a Crafty Croc

If you are making this drink for a party you can float a slice of strawberry on top to make it extra special.

Absolutely Apple Mint

Serves 2

Takes 5 mins

No cooking

(DB)

DF

GF

(V)

VG

WF

There is an old saying 'An apple a day keeps the doctor away' – nowadays we know that eating 5 portions of fresh fruit and vegetables a day helps to keep your body healthy.

Crafty Croc has lots of recipes for apples – this lovely refreshing drink is one of his favourites.

You Will Need

1 large apple
1 large ripe pear
a handful of fresh mint – spearmint is good
1 tbsp runny honey
1 tbsp crushed ice

blender or liquidiser
chopping board
sharp knife
potato peeler
tablespoon
tea towel
2 tall glasses
2 straws

Snap To It!

1 Using the potato peeler, peel the apple. Place it on the chopping board and carefully cut it into four pieces using the sharp knife. Then carefully cut out the core from each quarter.

2 Carefully cut the apple quarters into small squares about 1cm.

3 Peel, core and chop the pear on the chopping board in the same way you did the apple.

4 Pull off the little sprig from the top of the mint leaves and keep this for later.

5 Put all the ingredients, including the rest of the mint, into the blender (or liquidiser). Put on the lid – even old crocs forget to do this so make sure you place it on firmly. Put a tea towel over the lid to help you hold the blender steady while you switch it on. Be prepared in case the blender jumps a bit – this is caused by the fruit chunks and ice in the mixture.

6 Blend on slow to begin with and gradually increase the speed until the mixture is smooth and creamy.

7 Pour into the two glasses and decorate the top with the little mint sprig. Pop in your straw and serve.

Be a Crafty Croc

Diabetics and **Vegans** – miss out the honey.

Mulled Juices

This drink is great for a special party when the weather is colder.

The lovely spicy smells make you feel that Santa Claus is not far away!

You Will Need

1 litre carton of white grape juice
1 litre carton red grape juice
1 small carton (150ml) fresh orange juice
1 small carton (150ml) fresh apple juice
1 cinnamon stick
4 cloves
2 tsp runny honey

Decoration
10 slices of orange – cut in half

large pan
large wooden spoon
sharp knife
chopping board
mugs to serve

Snap To It!

1 Place the orange on the chopping board and use the sharp knife to trim off the top and bottom.

2 Holding the end of the orange in one hand, start at the opposite end and use the sharp knife to cut the orange into slices across the middle. Be careful to keep fingers well out of the way!

3 Place the large pan on the hob.

4 Pour in all the juices and then add the spices (cinnamon and cloves) and the honey.

5 Stir the mixture well with the wooden spoon, being careful to hold the handle of the pan with your other hand.

6 Turn on the heat to medium and cook until you see steam beginning to rise from the surface of the juice in the pan. This means that the juice is just warm and not too hot.

7 Turn off the heat.

8 Carefully pour the warm juice into mugs, pop 2 slices of orange on top and serve.

Be a Crafty Croc

Why not make double this amount and leave half to cool, then you can make it into Chilled Christmas Fizz later . . . (see the next page).

- **Diabetics** and **Vegans** – leave out the honey.

101

Chilled Christmas Fizz

Serves 10

Takes 30 mins

(DB)

DF

GF

(V)

VG

WF

This is a perfect drink for Christmas and will put a little more sparkle into the Festive Season!

You Will Need

1 quantity of Mulled Juices, cold
1 bottle of fizzy spring water
2 red apples
1 orange
ice cubes
(make some in funny shapes if you have a mould)

large bowl
soup ladle
sharp knife
chopping board
tall glasses

Gorgeous Glasses

1 Use a clean finger to rub a little boiled (and cooled) water round the rims of some juice tumblers.
2 Turn one upside down on to a saucer of caster sugar and twist it round so that the sugar sticks to the water.

Snap To It !

1 Wash and dry the fruit.

2 Place the apple on the chopping board. Use the sharp knife to cut it in half, from top to bottom.

3 Cut the halves in two along the length to make four quarters.

4 Cut round the core to remove it. Then carefully slice the quarters into thin slices. Place the slices into the bowl.

5 Place the orange on the chopping board and use the sharp knife to trim off the top and bottom.

6 Holding the end of the orange in one hand, start at the opposite end and use the sharp knife to cut the orange into slices across the middle. Be careful to keep fingers well out of the way!

7 Add the orange slices to the apple in the bowl.

8 Pour in the mulled juices and then top up with the fizzy water until you like the taste.

9 Drop in some ice, pour into glasses using the ladle and serve.

Be a Crafty Croc

Diabetics and **Vegans** – leave out the honey when you are making Mulled Juices.

3 Shake off the excess and leave to dry to give the effect of frost round the top of the juice tumblers.

Try this with your glasses too – carefully!
Why not add a little food colouring to the sugar –
have pink, green, blue or yellow rims!

Old-fashioned Orangeade

This is an old, old recipe which Crafty Croc's grandmother used to make. It still tastes as good today, especially when it is made fresh.

If you like lemons, try the next recipe. It's for Traditional Lemonade and tastes just as good!

You Will Need

2 oranges
1 lemon
110g (4oz) sugar
570ml (1 pint) boiling water

1 litre (1¾ pint) heat-proof jug
wooden spoon
grater
lemon squeezer
small sieve
measuring jug
plate to cover the jug
knife
glasses

Snap To It!

1 Wash and dry the oranges and lemon. Grate the rind on to a plate and scrape it into the jug. Wash and dry the plate.

2 Cut the fruit in half and squeeze out the juice using the lemon squeezer (see page 11).

3 Pour the juice into the jug being careful to remove any lemon pips.

4 Mix in the sugar.

5 Slowly and carefully, pour in the boiling water, stirring with the wooden spoon until the sugar has dissolved.

6 Stir with the wooden spoon and cover with the plate.

7 Leave to cool.

8 When the lemonade is cold, strain it through the small sieve into the measuring jug and leave to drain for 10 minutes. Throw the rind away.

9 Dilute to taste with cold water or fizzy spring water and serve.

Be a Crafty Croc

Keep the lemonade covered in the fridge and use within 3 days. This is a good drink to soothe a sore throat – just mix it with some hot water and a little honey.

Traditional Lemonade

There's nothing old fashioned about this – try it and see!

Serves 8

Takes 3 hours (or make the day before)

No cooking

DF

GF

V

VG

WF

You Will Need

2 large lemons
4oz (110g) castor sugar
1 pint boiling water

1 litre (1¾ pint) heat-proof jug
wooden spoon
grater
lemon squeezer
small sieve
measuring jug
plate to cover the jug
knife
glasses

Snap To It!

1 Wash and dry the lemons. Grate the rind off the lemons with the grater into the heat-proof jug.

2 Squeeze out the juice (see page 11) into the jug.

3 Mix in the sugar.

4 Carefully, pour in the boiling water, stirring with the wooden spoon until the sugar has dissolved.

5 Stir with the wooden spoon and cover with the plate.

6 Cover and leave to cool. Then chill in the fridge.

7 Strain through a sieve and serve cold, diluted to taste with sparkling spring water.

Su's Summer Woosh

A taste of summer all the year round.

You Will Need

1 litre bottle sparkling spring water
concentrated fruit juice of your choice
(1 to 2 tbsp per person)
1 kiwi fruit – sliced
4 black + 4 green seedless grapes
ice

tablespoon
4 cocktail sticks
4 tall glasses

Snap To It!

1 Drop two chunks of ice into each of the 4 glasses.

2 Pour over the fruit juice.

3 Top up with sparkling water – pour slowly or it will fizz up all over everything!

4 Thread a slice of kiwi fruit on to a cocktail stick. Then push on a green grape and a black grape. Lay the cocktail sticks flat on top of a glass.

5 Do the same with the other cocktail sticks.

6 If you have fresh strawberries, chop up a few and add to the drinks just before serving. Putting chopped strawberries in drinks is very popular in Germany where this drink comes from.

Fabulous Fizzing Fruit
Fantasy

This is a yummy way to eat fruit. Suss out the way to make it and then invent your own version.

A cross between a pudding and a drink.
– A puddink!

You Will Need

1 ripe banana – peeled
2 (dark) chocolate Matchmakers
110g (4oz) strawberries
4 dessertspoons vanilla ice cream
lemonade
1 tsp lemon juice

blender or liquidiser
saucer
2 tall glasses
2 straws
dessertspoon
teaspoon
chopping board
sharp knife

Snap To It!

1. Place the peeled banana on the chopping board and use the sharp knife to cut off 4 thin slices.

2. Pour a teaspoon of lemon juice into the saucer and toss the banana pieces in the lemon juice.

3. Push two banana pieces on to each Matchmaker.

4. Keep one strawberry for decoration and then put the rest of the strawberries and the rest of the banana into the blender (or liquidiser).

5. Put on the lid tightly and then blend on a slow speed until smooth.

6. Put 1 dessertspoon of ice cream in the bottom of each of the glasses.

7. Pour a quarter of the fruit mixture on top of the ice cream.

8. Top with another spoon of ice cream and, finally, pour in the rest of the fruit.

9. Very carefully (if you pour too quickly you will have an explosion of fizz) pour the lemonade into each glass until it reaches the top.

10. Carefully, use the sharp knife to cut the strawberry in half on the chopping board.

11. Float one half strawberry on top of each drink, stick the Matchmaker and the straw into the glass and get drinking!

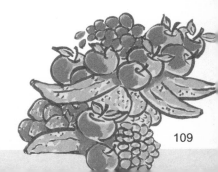

Witch's Brew

This is a perfect recipe for Hallowe'en or anytime you feel like an exciting drink.

Serves 6

Takes 10 mins

Needs freezing (2 hours)

No cooking

DF

GF

VG

WF

You Will Need

2 cartons fresh apple juice
1 bottle green food colouring
1 packet sweetie shoelaces (black or green are best)
1 bottle sparkling water

ice cube tray or ice cube bag
jug
wooden spoon
6 tall glasses

Snap To It!

1 Pour 300ml (½ pint) apple juice into the jug.

2 Mix in a few drops of green colouring – add a little at a time until you get a colour you like.

3 Stir with the wooden spoon

4 Pour the juice into the ice cube tray and leave to set hard in the freezer.

5 Decorate the glasses with the shoelaces.

6 When the ice cubes are ready, half fill each glass with apple juice and top up with sparkling water. Pop in a few ice cubes and watch the Witch's Brew develop as the ice melts into the juice!

Sweet Sensations

Sometimes we really feel like something sweet. Fabulous fruit comes in all shapes and sizes – fresh, dried and canned – and makes some lovely yummy things to eat. Enjoy the Sweet Sensation adventure!

Sundae on a Monday

Serves 2

Takes 10 mins

Cook – microwave

(DF)

GF

VG

WF

This is a tasty pudding for any day of the week. Ice cream sundaes can be as extravagant as you like.

Anything goes – be outrageous!

You Will Need

4 scoops of any ice cream of your choice
a handful of banana chips
chocolate chips
1 fruit bar (apple and strawberry tastes good) take your pick

poly bag
chopping board
wooden spoon
sharp knife
bowl
tablespoon
2 tall glasses or sundae dishes
ice-cream scoop

Snap To It!

1 Put the banana chips into a poly bag and close the top tightly.

2 Place the bag on a chopping board and it a good whack with a wooden spoon to break the banana chips into smaller pieces. Set the bag to one side.

3 Place the fruit bar on the chopping board and use the sharp knife to carefully chop the fruit bar into small bits.

4 Place the fruit bar bits into a bowl and add 1 tablespoon of cold water. Microwave on high for 20 seconds, stir well and then leave to soak for a few minutes while you make up the pudding.

5 Drop a scoop or large scoop of ice cream into the foot of two tall glasses or sundae dishes, sprinkle with banana chips and chocolate chips then top with another large dollop of ice cream.

6 Stir your hot fruit sauce well – add more hot water if it is thick and then pour the hot melted fruit bar over the concoction.

7 Serve at once – the hot fruit makes the drink all gooey and very yummy. It is a sensation not to be missed – which is what will happen if you do not eat your Sundae right away!!

Be a Crafty Croc

To make this a **Dairy Free** recipe, use dairy-free ice cream and special chocolate chips.

Creamy Caramel Crisp

The correct name for this is actually Fruit Brulee – 'brulee' means burnt. If you are careful you should have a nice caramel topping – and not a burnt cinder!

Different sugars will give you different caramel tastes – try castor, granulated or demerara. Remember, white sugar burns more easily than brown so watch it even more carefully!

You Will Need

1 large pot (450g) thick creamy yoghurt
(or fromage frais – natural or vanilla is best)
soft brown sugar

Fruit of your choice . . .
strawberries, raspberries, chopped peaches or apple (but not oranges and mandarines – they will make the topping curdle!)

1 large oven-proof dish or 4 small ones
sieve
sharp knife
chopping board
baking tray
oven gloves

Snap To It!

1 Choose 1 large oven-proof dish or 4 small ones.

2 Sliced or chop the fruit on the chopping board with the sharp knife (see page 10).

3 Spread the fruit over the bottom of the dishes.

4 Cover all the fruit with the thick yoghurt or fromage frais.

5 Turn on the grill to heat at high.

6 Use the sieve to shake a layer of soft brown sugar over the top of the yoghurt or fromage frais to completely cover it. Make sure that there is no white showing at all – the sugar layer is there to protect the pudding underneath, just like a blanket.

7 Put your dish or dishes on to a baking tray. Use oven gloves to carefully slide it under the hot grill.

8 The grill will heat the sugar layer on top of your pudding so that it melts to caramel – it can easily burn so you must watch it all the time. The caramel is ready when all the sugar has melted but is not burned.

9 When the sugar melts, darkens in colour and begins to bubble use your oven gloves to remove the baking tray at once and set it on a heat-resistant surface.

10 Now you have a choice – allow to cool a little and eat while warm on top and cool underneath, or chill in the fridge and let the caramel turn hard and crispy. The decision is yours!

Be a Crafty Croc

Use soya yoghurt instead of the normal stuff to make this a **Dairy Free** recipe.

You can use tinned or frozen fruit in this recipe – just make sure you drain away as much juice as possible and keep the juice to make a nice drink.

Fruit Parcels

These are so simple! Parcels are great for barbecues, parties or just for a treat at home.

This is the sort of pudding that you invent as you go along – depending on what you find in the fruit bowl or cupboard. You can use fresh or dried fruit, but avoid fruit with lots of stones or seeds – you will have lots of funny bits when it is cooked!

Have a parcel-making party and ask guests to make their own!

You Will Need

all or any of these (chopped or sliced) . . .

fresh fruits . . .
peaches · nectarines · strawberries · apples
pears · plums · bananas

dried fruits . . .
apricots · sultanas · raisins · apples · pitted prunes

meusli – your favourite
1 tbsp concentrated fresh fruit juice – any flavour
marshmallows or broken chocolate pieces

aluminium foil or baking parchment
sharp knife
chopping board
tablespoon
baking tray
oven gloves

Snap To It!

1 Arrange the shelves in the oven so the baking tray can sit on the middle shelf. Turn on the oven to heat at Gas 6, 400°F or 200°C.

2 Choose your own selection of fruit – add banana or dried fruit to give the parcel a nice sweet taste. Place the fruit on the chopping board and chop with the sharp knife (see page 10).

3 If you are going to cook the parcels in the oven, take a square of foil big enough to hold a quarter of the fruit and lay it flat on the table. Use baking parchment instead of foil if you are going to cook the parcels in the microwave.

4 Place the fruit in the centre of the square and drizzle 1 tablespoon of fruit juice over the fruit.

5 Sprinkle with meusli and top with a few pieces of chocolate or marshmallow.

6 Wrap the foil or baking parchment tightly round the fruit, making sure that there are no holes for the liquid to escape.

7 Do the same with the other squares of foil or baking parchment.

IN THE OVEN

a) Lay the parcels on a baking tray and use the oven gloves to carefully place it in the pre-heated oven. Cook for 15 minutes.

b) Use oven gloves to take the hot tray out of the oven and place it on a heat-resistant surface.

IN THE MICROWAVE

a) Place the parcels in the microwave and cook on high power for 3 to 4 minutes, depending on the quantity of fruit in the parcel.

b) Use oven gloves to lift the parcel on to a heat-resistant surface.

Be a Clever Croc

Safety first – let the fruit parcels cool a little, then open carefully. The steam from the cooked fruit can be VERY hot. If in doubt, ask an adult to help – just to open and not to eat!

Choc-a-Dunk!

This is a tantalising tongue treat for a party or for after a family meal. You can dip many different fruits into this delicious pool of melted chocolate. Choose from the list at the end of the recipe.

Dark chocolate should be fine for Dairy Frees and those who cannot eat wheat, but be smart and check the label to be sure.

You Will Need

225g (8oz) plain dark chocolate
2 tbsp golden syrup
2 large bananas
150ml (½ pint) cream (or dairy-free alternative)
2 tbsp apple juice

chopping board
sharp knife
flat plate
saucepan
fork
wooden spoon
tablespoon
forks or cocktail sticks
(one for each person)
serving bowl

Snap To It!

1 Peel the bananas and chop them up on the chopping board. Place them in the bowl and mash with the fork.

2 Add the cream or dairy-free alternative to the mashed banana and mix well with the fork.

3 Place the chocolate on the chopping board and cut it into small pieces with the sharp knife.

4 Put the pieces of chocolate into the saucepan and add the syrup and apple juice.

5 Add the banana and cream mixture to the chocolate in the pan.

6 Put the pan on the hob and turn the heat to medium. Let the mixture heat through, stirring a few times with the wooden spoon, but DO NOT let it boil.

7 Carefully take the pan off the heat and set on a heat-resistant surface. Let it cool slightly and then carefully pour the mixture into the serving bowl. Now place whatever dippers you have chosen on to the forks or cocktail sticks and tuck in!

Be a Crafty Croc

Here are plenty of dipper ideas –

Fruit
• plums • raspberries •
• strawberries • grapes • dates • cherries •
• chunks of apple or pear •

Sweeties
• jelly babies •
• marshmallows • toffee chunks •

119

Veronica's Apple Pudding

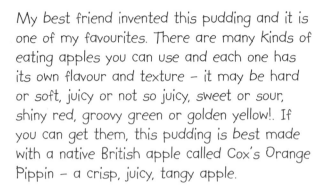

Serves 2

Takes 10 mins

No cooking

(DB)

(DF)

GF

(V)

VG

WF

My best friend invented this pudding and it is one of my favourites. There are many kinds of eating apples you can use and each one has its own flavour and texture – it may be hard or soft, juicy or not so juicy, sweet or sour, shiny red, groovy green or golden yellow!. If you can get them, this pudding is best made with a native British apple called Cox's Orange Pippin – a crisp, juicy, tangy apple.

This pudding has to be eaten straight away, but that's okay – once you have made it, you won't want to wait!

You Will Need

3 large Cox's apples (or Braeburn or Gala)
1 tbsp soft brown sugar
1 tbsp chopped nuts (or banana chips)
1 small carton of single cream

grater
plate
sharp knife
potato peeler
chopping board
bowl
spoon
2 dessert bowls

Snap To It !

1 Using the potato peeler, peel the apples. Place an apple on the chopping board and carefully cut it into four pieces using the sharp knife. Then carefully cut out the core from each quarter.

2 Do the same with the other apples.

3 Use the roughest side of the grater to grate an apple quarter into the bowl. Be careful of your fingers, as the grater can be very sharp.

4 Grate the other pieces of apple. Use a spoon to scrape off all the apple from the grater.

5 Divide the grated apple between the two dessert bowls.

6 Sprinkle the soft brown sugar and nuts or banana chips over the grated apple.

7 Pour a thin stream of cream over the top and eat at once.

Be a Crafty Croc

- If you are **sensitive to nuts**, use crushed dried banana chips or biscuit crumbs instead (the best ones are digestive biscuits). Put the banana chips or biscuits into a poly bag, make sure it is fastened shut and then bash the contents with a wooden spoon or rolling pin to make crumbs. If you are also **Gluten Free** – use crushed dried banana chips or gluten-free biscuit crumbs instead of nuts.

- To make this recipe for someone who eats a **Dairy Free** or **Vegan** diet, miss out the cream and use fresh apple juice or rice cream instead.

- **Diabetics** – miss out the sugar and add a handful of raisins instead.

Juicy Baked Apple

Serves 1

Takes 40 mins

Cook – oven

DB

DF

(GF)

(V)

(VG)

(WF)

The *best* apples to choose for this are large cooking apples – Bramleys are good because they are the fluffiest when *baked*.

There are lots of fillings you can put into the middle of apples . . .

• soft brown sugar • syrup •
• raisins • jam • sweets •

Why not make this as a change from Christmas Pudding!

You Will Need

1 jar of mincemeat (wheat free or vegan)
1 large Bramley cooking apple

potato peeler or apple corer
chopping board
sharp knife
flat Pyrex dish
teaspoon
large serving spoon
oven gloves

Snap To It!

1 Arrange the shelves in the oven so the baking tray can sit on the middle shelf. Turn on the oven to heat at Gas 6, 400°F or 200°C.

2 Wash and dry the apple.

3 Put the apple on the chopping board and hold it steady with one hand. With your other hand, dig the potato peeler or apple corer into the apple round the core. The peeler may not be able to cut out the core in one go, so you will have to move it gradually round the core until you have cut all round it. Then press with your thumbs to push the core out of the apple.

4 Use the sharp knife to cut through the skin round the middle of the apple – this prevents the apple exploding as it cooks inside. Just cut through the skin, don't go all the way through the apple.

5 Put the apple on to the Pyrex dish.

6 Use the teaspoon to put the mincemeat into the hole where the apple core was. Push the mincemeat well down with the teaspoon and keep doing this until the core part is filled up.

7 Pour a little water into the dish and use the oven gloves to carefully place the dish into the oven. Bake for 20 to 30 minutes, depending on the size of your apple, until it is soft and squishy.

8 Use the oven gloves to take the dish from the oven and set on a heat-resistant surface. Use the large serving spoon to lift the apple into a pudding bowl.

9 Leave to cool a little before eating. Serve with custard sauce, ice cream, cream, yoghurt or just eat it on its own. Lovely!

Be a Crafty Croc

- **Diabetics**, **Vegetarians** and **Vegans** – use a mixture of raisins sultanas and chopped dates instead of mincemeat. Add a good pinch of mixed spice to give the fruit mixture more taste.
- **Dairy Free** and **Vegan** – serve with dairy-free ice cream.

Baked Bananas

This is one of Crafty's favourite puddings, especially when he goes camping. He likes to bake his bananas in the ashes of the campfire and eat them warm, sitting by the fire.

Baked Bananas can be cooked in the oven or the microwave and you can even even pop your foil wrapped banana on to the barbecue!

Serves 1

Takes 20 mins

Cook – oven
(or microwave
or barbecue)

(DF)

(GF)

(V)

VG

WF

You Will Need

1 ripe banana

Filling
strawberry jam or marshmallows
or your favourite mini-chocolate bar
(check the label to make sure it suits your diet)

chopping board
spoon
sharp knife
aluminium foil or baking parchment
baking tray
oven gloves

Be a Crafty Croc

Dairy Free and **Vegan** – go for dark chocolate.

Snap To It !

1 If you are going to cook the parcels in the oven, arrange the shelves in the oven so the baking tray can sit on the middle shelf. Turn on the oven to heat at Gas 6, 400°F or 200°C.

2 If you are going to cook the bananas in the oven, take a square of foil big enough to to wrap round the banana and lay it flat on the table. Use baking parchment instead of foil if you are going to cook the bananas in the microwave.

3 Place the banana on the chopping board and use the point of the sharp knife to make a slit along the length of the banana. Cut through the flesh but don't go through the skin at the other side.

4 Lift the banana on to middle of the foil or baking parchment squares.

5 Gently, using your thumbs as levers, open the slit to make a pocket. You can put any sweet thing you like into this pocket. Try strawberry jam, marshmallows or chocolate. Dried fruit and mincemeat are good at Christmas time.

6 Now close the pocket up as best you can – this may be difficult if you have a lot of filling!

7 Now wrap the foil or baking parchment round the banana, making sure that there are no holes.

IN THE OVEN

a) Place the parcel on to a baking tray and use the oven gloves to carefully place it in the pre-heated oven. Bake for 15 minutes.

b) Use oven gloves to take the hot tray out of the oven and place it on a heat-resistant surface. Leave to cool a little.

IN THE MICROWAVE

a) Place the parcel in the microwave and cook on high power for 2 minutes. Leave to cool for 1 minute as it will be very hot.

8 Use oven gloves to lift the parcel on to a plate. Open it away from your face so that the escaping hot steam doesn't burn you.

Cool Banana Split

Serves 4

Takes 10 mins

No cooking

(DF)

GF

(V)

VG

(WF)

A must for the summer. This recipe features home-made fresh strawberry sauce – guaranteed to impress your friends and family!

This pudding needs to be made just before you are going to eat it. The strawberry sauce is also great in fruit parcels, baked bananas, yoghurt and on ice cream.

You Will Need

4 ripe bananas
ice cream (any flavour)
225g (8oz) fresh strawberries
1 tube of aerosol cream – reduced fat
1 tsp icing sugar
chocolate vermicelli

sieve
bowl
teaspoon
wooden spoon
chopping board
sharp knife
ice-cream scoop or large spoon
4 long narrow dishes
(sundae dishes or corn on the cob dishes)
damp cloth

Snap To It!

1 Peel the bananas.

2 Place one banana on the chopping board and use the point of the sharp knife to cut along the length of the banana. Put both halves into a long dish with the cut side facing up; place them at an angle to form a v-shape. This will act like a dish to hold the ice cream.

3 Do the same with the other bananas.

4 Place the strawberries in a sieve, hold it under the tap and run cold water over the strawberries to wash them. Drain them well and dry the sieve.

5 Lay the bowl on a damp cloth to prevent it from sliding around.

6 Put the sieve over the bowl and then pour in the fresh strawberries. Hold the sieve in one hand and the wooden spoon in your other hand. Using the back of the wooden spoon, push the fruit through the holes in the sieve so that all juice and flesh runs into the bowl.

7 Push through as much fruit as you can, then use the wooden spoon to scrape the rest of the strawberry sticking to the underside of the sieve. Put the sieve into the sink.

8 Stir the icing sugar into the strawberry mash until it has all dissolved.

9 Put two scoops or spoons of ice cream into each banana dish.

10 Pour a spoon of strawberry sauce over the ice cream.

11 Scoosh a dollop of cream on top and sprinkle with chocolate vermicelli. Serve and enjoy!

Be a Crafty Croc

Dairy Free or **Vegan**? Leave out the aerosol cream and use dairy-free ice cream! There are some delicious flavours to choose from. My favourite is strawberry. Yum!

Banana Boat

Serves 1

Takes 10 mins

Needs
freezing
(1 hour)

No cooking

DB

(DF)

GF

(V)

VG

WF

Bananas are one of the best snack foods you will find. Bananas are better than sweets or chocolate, which give you a huge amount of energy quickly, but in a short time your body will need more.

Athletes and other people who need a lot of energy for physical work eat bananas to give them quick and sustained, or long-lasting, energy so,

Go Bananas!

You Will Need

1 banana
carton of strawberry yoghurt
(or soya yoghurt)
4 fresh strawberries

plastic freezer tub or tray
chopping board
sharp knife
plate or long serving dish
teaspoon
fork
spoon

Snap To It!

1 Peel the banana.

2 Place the banana on the chopping board and use the point of the sharp knife to cut along the length of the banana.

3 Put both halves into a plastic tray and place in the deep freeze for about 1 hour.

4 While the banana is freezing, wash and dry the strawberries. Place them on the chopping board and carefully use the sharp knife to slice them up.

5 After an hour, lift the tray out of the freezer and carefully lift each banana half on to a long serving dish. Make sure that the cut side is facing upwards.

6 Smother in yoghurt. Use a teaspoon to get all the yoghurt out of its pot.

7 Scatter the sliced strawberries on top.

8 Leave for a few minutes – the yoghurt will get very cold and will turn thick. The strawberries will begin to melt!

9 Serve with a fork and spoon as the banana will be a little hard to start with. This tastes very, very good on a hot day.

Be a Crafty Croc

Try using other fruit, like peach halves, instead of bananas.

Make life easy – use canned fruit in juice. Drain the fruit by emptying the tin into a sieve placed over a bowl. The bowl will catch the juice which you can drink later!

Chocolate Banana Roll-over

This recipe uses banana and chocolate, but you can also try –

grated apple, raisins and chocolate chips

or

crushed strawberries and chopped grapes.

Make this recipe really posh with a very crafty trick – read on!

You Will Need

4 ready-made crepes (page 80)
(or large thin pancakes)
2 ripe bananas
1 packet of chocolate chips
cocoa powder

bowl
small sieve
teaspoon
fork
knife
4 white flat plates
knife and fork

Snap To It !

1 Peel the bananas and put them into the bowl. Mash them well with the fork until they are creamy.

2 Stir in 2 teaspoons of cocoa powder.

3 Add half of the packet of chocolate chips.

4 Lay a crepe or pancake on each plate and divide the filling between each. Spreading the filling over half of the crepe or pancake only.

5 Fold the other half of the crepe or pancake over the filling to make a half circle shape and scatter some of the chocolate chips on top.

6 Put one pancake half on each plate. Now for the trick – you have to be careful – arrange the knife and fork at each side of a pancake half on the plate.

7 Hold the sieve over the pancake and knife and fork. Use the teaspoon to drop a little cocoa powder into the sieve and shake it over the pancake and knife and fork.

8 Lay the sieve and teaspoon down. Then very carefully lift the knife and fork from the plate and – hey presto! – you will find a very professional pattern.

9 Wash the knife and fork and repeat this with all the other plates.

10 Serve and amaze your friends!

Be a Crafty Croc

Once you have made this pattern you can do it again with other puddings – try icing sugar instead of cocoa.

- **Gluten Free + Wheat Free** – use special pancakes.
- **Dairy Free** – use dark chocolate chips.
- **Diabetic + Vegan** – miss out the chocolate chips

Kiwi Surprise

Surprisingly good for you!

Serves 2

Takes 10 mins

No cooking

DB

VG

You Will Need

1 kiwi fruit
1 carton strawberry yoghurt (low fat)
1 biscuit (shortbread or digestive)
1 can aerosol cream (low fat)
cocoa powder

potato peeler
chopping board
sharp knife
large bowl
wooden spoon
sieve
2 dishes

Snap To It!

1 Use the potato peeler to peel the kiwi fruit.

2 Place the kiwi fruit on the chopping board, chop it up with the sharp knife and put the pieces into a large bowl.

3 Pour in the yoghurt.

4 Break the biscuit into pieces and add them to the yoghurt mixture. Mix well with the wooden spoon.

5 Spoon into two dishes and scoosh a neat rose of cream on top of each serving.

6 Sieve and shake a little cocoa powder over the top and serve.

Melba Sandwich

A simple version of a posh pud.

Serves 2

Takes 10 mins

No cooking

(DF)

(V)

VG

You Will Need

4 biscuits (shortbread or digestive)
1 ripe peach (or nectarine)
1 jar raspberry jam (or strawberry jam)
ice cream (or yoghurt)

potato peeler
knife for spreading
plate
sharp knife
chopping board

Snap To It !

1 Use the potato peeler to peel the peach.

2 Set the peach on the chopping board, cut round the stone with the sharp knife and place it flat side down. Carefully slice up the flesh.

3 Spread two biscuits with a thick layer of jam.

4 Top with over-lapping slices of peach or nectarine and then place another biscuit on top to make a fruit sandwich.

5 Set the sandwich on a plate and pop it into the fridge for about 30 minutes to chill and soften the shortbread biscuit.

6 Serve cold with a scoop of vanilla ice cream or a dollop of yoghurt (use dairy-free ice cream or soya yoghurt for a dairy-free or vegan recipe).

Fruity Frog Spawn

Serves 4

Takes 1 hour
30 mins

Cook – oven

(DB)

DF

GF

V

WF

Tapioca looks like little beads and is made from the root of a plant called cassava, which grows in warmer places.

When it is cooked it looks a bit like frog spawn – but tastes much better!!

You Will Need

450g tin of strawberries in fruit juice
2 level tbsp tapioca
25g (1oz) sugar (optional)

1 litre (1¾ pint) pie dish
baking tray
aluminium foil
tin opener
oven gloves
tablespoon

Snap To It !

1 Arrange the shelves in the oven so the baking tray can sit on the middle shelf. Turn on the oven to heat at Gas 4, 350°F or 180°C.

2 Open the tin of fruit and pour it into the pie dish.

3 Sprinkle the tapioca (and sugar if you want it) over the top and mix it well into the fruit with the tablespoon.

4 Put the pie dish on to the baking tray and then cover the pie dish with aluminium foil.

5 Using the oven gloves, carefully lift the tray into the oven. Bake for 1 hour.

6 Using the oven gloves, carefully remove the tray from the oven and set on to a heat-resistant surface. Leave to cool a little.

7 Very carefully open the foil – open it away from you so that the escaping steam will not burn you.

8 Serve hot with custard, ice cream or yoghurt, or leave till cool and then chill in the fridge to enjoy cold.

Be a Crafty Croc

Choose any fruit you like –

* raspberries *

* blackberries *

* peaches *

* mandarines *

or something exotic like mangoes!!

* **Diabetics** – miss out the sugar and make sure you use fruits canned in fruit juice.
* **Dairy Free** – use dairy-free ice cream, yoghurt or a cream substitute.

Sea Food, Eat Food

Serves 4

Takes 45 mins
(2 hours to set
or leave
overnight)

Cook – hob

DB

(DF)

GF

(V)

VG

WF

Carageen is a seaweed – brownish purple in colour – used hundreds of years ago to make jelly like puddings long before the Scots knew anything about gelatine.

You don't need to use very much to make this tasty dish which, as well as being delicious, is very good for you too.

You Will Need

12g (½ oz) dried carageen
570ml (1 pint) milk (or soya milk
or other substitute)
25g (1oz) sugar
few drops vanilla essence
(or milkshake syrup)

saucepan
bowl
wooden spoon
sieve
serving bowl or jelly mould

Snap To It !

1 Put the carageen into the sieve and hold under cold running water for a few minutes to wash.

2 Shake well to drain it and tip the carageen into the pan.

3 Pour in the milk, sugar and vanilla essence.

4 Place the pan on the hob and turn the heat to medium. Hold the handle of the pan in one hand and, with the wooden spoon in the other hand, stir the mixture until it comes to the boil.

5 Turn down the heat to low and leave to cook very slowly for about 15 minutes until the seaweed is soft and the milk is thick. Leaving the wooden spoon in the pan helps to prevent the milk boiling over and making a mess!

6 Take the pan off the heat and set on a heat-resistant surface.

7 Put the sieve over the bowl and carefully pour the milk mixture into the sieve. This will strain out the seaweed and leave your tasty pudding in the bowl.

8 Carefully, pour the milky liquid into a nice bowl or jelly mould and then place in a cool place to set.

9 Serve. This is good to eat alone and it's great with All Day Breakfast (see page 70) sprinkled on top or with a bowl of fresh strawberries.

Be a Crafty Croc

Make a pink pud – add a few drops of red food colouring!

McScoff's Pud

Serves 2

Takes 30 mins

Cook – oven
(or microwave)

DB

DF

(V)

VG

Have you ever gone berrying and ended up with purple hands, tongue and face? Proof that fruit can *be* FUN!

Brambles and Blaeberries taste great mixed with apples – try this one for size!

You Will Need

4 tbsp of cooked stewed apples
50g (2oz) brambles (or blaeberries,
strawberries or raspberries)
1 tbsp rolled oats
1 x 50g pack of meusli
(dairy free)

oven or microwave proof dish
oven gloves

Snap To It !

1 If you are going to cook this in the oven, arrange the shelves in the oven so the oven-proof dish can sit on the middle shelf. Turn on the oven to heat at Gas 4, 350°F or 180°C.

2 Put the fruits into the bottom of the oven-proof dish.

3 Sprinkle the oats on top.

4 Sprinkle the meusli on top.

5 Now to cook –

   IN THE OVEN

   Use the oven gloves to place the dish in the hot oven. Bake for 20 minutes.

   IN THE MICROWAVE

   Place the dish in the microwave and cook on high power for 1 minute.

6 Use oven gloves to take the hot dish out of the oven and place it on a heat-resistant surface. Leave to cool a little.

7 Serve with natural yoghurt or rice dream for a Dairy Free pudding.

Be a Crafty Croc

Instead of brambles you can add raisins, sultanas or chopped dates to the apples.

Try other stewed fruits like rhubarb or plums instead of apples.

Mmmmmama Monster

Make a monster and have a

monster munch!

Yumscious!

How many new words can you invent to describe new tastes?

You Will Need

250g (8oz) packet ginger nut biscuits
1 medium carton thick Greek yoghurt
(or fromage frais)
2 black grapes
1 large fresh strawberry

sharp knife
chopping board
knife for spreading
long, flat serving plate
aluminium foil or cling film
small sieve

Snap To It!

1 Cut a piece of foil or cling film large enough to wrap the packet of biscuits in, leaving plenty of room.

2 Lift a biscuit in one hand and the spreading knife in the other. Spread one side of the biscuit with the yoghurt or fromage frais.

3 Lift another biscuit, stick it on to the yoghurt or fromage frais and spread the empty side with more yoghurt or fromage frais.

4 Keep spreading and sticking on biscuits until you have used up all the biscuits and made a long biscuit roll, like a snake.

5 Set the biscuit roll on the foil or cling film.

6 Spread the rest of the yoghurt or fromage frais all over the biscuit roll.

7 Wrap the foil or cling film tightly round the biscuit roll and place in the fridge to chill overnight.

8 The next day, wash and dry the grapes and the strawberry.

9 Place the strawberry on the chopping board and use the sharp knife to cut it in half.

10 Take the biscuit roll out of the fridge and carefully roll the monster out of the wrapping and on to the plate.

11 Stick on the grapes for the eyes and use the strawberry for a nose and mouth – stick the cut side on to the end of the roll to make a nose and stick the cut side facing out to make a mouth.

Be a Crafty Croc

- Make sure you use special biscuits if you want to make a **Gluten** and **Wheat Free** recipe.
- **Dairy Free** and **Vegan** – use dairy-free yoghurt, and check that the biscuits are also dairy free.

Here are **2** chocolate cakes for you to try. The first is wheat and gluten free, the second contains no dairy products! Something for everyone!

Irmhild's Chocolate Cake

Serves 6

Takes 1 hour

Bake – oven

GF

VG

WF

You Will Need

4 eggs
150g castor sugar
150g butter
80g chocolate flakes
75g gluten-free breadcrumbs (or biscuit crumbs)
150g ground hazelnuts (or almonds)
1 tsp gluten-free baking powder
vegetable oil

mixing bowl
pastry brush
wooden spoon
baking tin (18cm x 28cm)
whisk
greaseproof paper
oven gloves
cooling rack
skewer or sharp knife
serving plate – something posh!

Snap To It !

1 Arrange the shelves in the oven so the baking tin can sit on the middle shelf. Turn on the oven to heat at Gas 4, 350°F or 180°C.

2 Grease and line the baking tin with greaseproof paper.

   a) Lay the tin on a sheet of greaseproof paper, draw round the base and cut out the shape. Cut out a piece to fit around the side of the tin as well.

   b) Brush a little vegetable oil round the inside of the tin. Stick the grease paper pieces to the bottom and sides of the tin.

   c) Brush all over the paper with oil.

3 Put the butter and sugar into the mixing bowl and beat well together until the mixture is fluffy.

4 Separate the eggs (see page 18) and gradually add the yolks to the butter and sugar mixture, beating well with the wooden spoon all the time.

5 Stir in the nuts, crumbs, baking powder and chocolate flakes.

6 Beat the egg whites with the whisk until they are stiff (this may take a while!). Stir them very gently into the chocolate mixture.

7 Carefully pour the mixture into the prepared tin and then, wearing the oven gloves, place the tin into the oven.

8 Bake for 20 to 30 minutes until the cake has risen and become firm. Use the oven gloves to lift out the tin and set it on a heat-resistant surface.

9 Test to see if it is cooked with the point of a knife or skewer — push it into the middle of the cake, if it comes out clean the cake is ready. If the knife or skewer has cake mixture on it, then put it back in the oven to cook for another 10 minutes — remember to wear oven gloves!

10 Lift the cooked cake out of the oven using oven gloves and set it on a cooling rack. Leave the cake to cool in the tin.

11 Carefully, turn the tin upside down on the serving plate. Lift the tin so that the cake comes out to sit on the plate.

12 Serve.

Fiona's Dairy-Free Chocolate Cake

Serves 6

Takes 1 hour

Bake – oven

DF

V

VG

To make a very special cake, lay sliced strawberries on top. Drizzle with Strawberry Sauce (see page 126) and decorate with cream. Yum!

You Will Need

280g (10oz) self-raising flour
50g (2oz) cocoa powder
3 tsp baking powder
250g (9oz) vanilla sugar (or castor sugar)
9 tbsp sunflower oil
12 fl.oz (12 tbsp) water
1½ tsp vanilla essence
a little icing sugar

filling
banana – mash in a bowl and mix in a
sprinkling of cinnamon to taste
or
strawberries – crush them in a bowl with a fork and
mix in a little icing sugar and a dash of vanilla

2 x 16cm sandwich tins
mixing bowl
wooden spoon
greaseproof paper
cooling rack
sieve
palette knife
oven gloves

Snap To It !

1 Turn on the oven to heat at Gas 3, 325F or 170°C.

2 Grease two sandwich tins about 16cm wide (see page 143).

3 Sift the flour, cocoa and baking powder together into a bowl.

4 Add the sugar, vanilla (if you like it), oil and water.

5 Mix well with the wooden spoon until it becomes thick and creamy (this is called a 'batter').

6 Pour half of the mixture into each of the tins. You may need to shake the tins gently to spread the mixture evenly.

7 Wearing the oven gloves, place the tin on the middle shelf of the oven to bake for about 40 minutes.

8 Lift one cake tin out of the oven with the oven gloves and set it on a heat-resistant surface. With a clean finger just press lightly in the middle — if it springs back, it is ready; if it is still feels soggy it is not. Bake for another 5 minutes and test again — remember to wear oven gloves!

9 When the cakes are cooked, lift them out of the oven using oven gloves and set the tins on a cooling rack. Leave for a few minutes to cool. Put your oven gloves back on. Run the palette knife round the inside of the tin to ease the cake away from the side of the tin. Carefully turn each tin upside down and lift it so that the cake comes out to sit on the cooling rack. Leave the cakes to cool.

10 While they are cooling, make up your filling (either with banana mashed with a sprinkling of cinnamon; or with crushed strawberries mixed with a little icing sugar and a dash of vanilla). Spread the filling on one cake half and set the other half on top to make a sandwich.

11 Sift a little icing sugar on to the top of the cake — to make a pattern lay a lacy doily on top of the cake first and then sift on the icing sugar. Carefully lift the doily and you will have a lovely pattern!

12 Serve with a cream substitute such as Elmlea or Rice Dream.

Arctic Explorer's Sweeties

Serves 4

Takes 5 mins

Needs
freezing
(2 hours)

No cooking

DB

DF

GF

V

VG

WF

Did you know that if bananas are left lying in a place that is cold enough for frost, they immediately turn black and become soggy and unpleasant!

So if you want to go exploring in the Arctic, don't carry a banana as a handy snack because you'll get a nasty surprise when you reach into your lunch box!!

Sporties, dairy frees and diabetics – this is the perfect snack for you on a hot summer day. Cool, refreshing and delicious!

You Will Need

4 large bananas

chopping board
sharp knife
freezer tray
freezer bag or container
cocktail sticks
sticky labels

Snap To It!

1 Peel the bananas.

2 Place one banana on the chopping board and use the sharp knife to cut it into pieces about 2cms long.

3 Do the same with the other bananas.

4 Lay these pieces flat on the freezer tray and then put a cocktail stick into each one.

5 Put the tray in the freezer and freeze for 2 hours.

6 After 2 hours take the tray out of the freezer. Quickly pop the banana pieces into a freezer bag or container, stick on a label (with the date you made them) and put them back in the freezer. You can keep the banana pieces in the freezer for up to 6 months.

These Sweeties taste like ice cream and are great alone or with a sauce. Invent your own or try Strawberry Sauce (see page 126) or make the recipes on the next page.

Grab a Grape

Use seedless grapes instead of banana. They taste like deep frozen sweeties – great for hot days and you can make your own! Remember to use seedless grapes and try and make sure that they are sweet and not sour – any size or colour will do.

1 Take the grapes off the stalk and wash them well under running cold water.

2 Dry them well with kitchen towel and place them on a freezer tray.

3 Put the tray into the freezer and wait for about 2 hours until frozen. Quickly pop them pour into a freezer box, label them and put them back in the freezer until you want them.

Cinnamon and Vanilla Yoghurt

DB
GF
VG
WF

Add 1 tsp **cinnamon** and a few drops of **vanilla essence** to a small tub of thick **natural yoghurt** and mix well. Serve chilled.

Hot Chocolate

GF
VG
WF

Break your favourite **chocolate** – milk, white or plain – into a bowl. Melt in the microwave on high power for 1 minute or over a pan of hot water on the hob. (Make sure the water is not touching the bottom of the bowl.) Use oven gloves to pour the chocolate into a serving dish and serve at once. It is good for dipping frozen banana pieces into (see page 146).

Honey and Strawberry Smoothie

DB
DF
GF
VG
WF

125g strawberries
½ ripe banana
2 tablespoons fresh fruit juice (apple or orange)
a drizzle of runny honey

Blitz all the ingredients in a food processor or a blender. Yum!

Party Time!

Party time is a great excuse to have fun with food. Try these recipes to impress your friends at birthday parties and family get-togethers, like Christmas.

Christmas is one of the biggest feasts of the year and adults shouldn't get all the fun! You can make tasty treats to eat and drink too! Just a little thought and a little preparation can make all the difference. Check the cupboards and fridge to make sure you have everything you need.

Traffic Fruity Lights

Serves lots of friends

Takes 30 mins

No cooking

(DF)

GF

(V)

VG

WF

Traffic lights are three different colours:

1. Red – for stop
2. Amber – to get ready
3. Green – to go

Fruit and vegetables come in all different colours and it is easy to make many versions of these 'traffic light kebabs'. They are made by threading small pieces of fruit, vegetables, cheese, meat, poultry or fish on to sticks called 'skewers'. Sometimes they are cooked, but Croc likes his to be as easy as 1–2–3!

You Will Need

Fruit
1 small tub fresh strawberries
1 bunch seedless green grapes
1 tin pineapple chunks
(or peach slices) in fruit juice

Dip
1 tub creamy vanilla yoghurt
(low fat)
or
1 tub natural fruit spread
(dairy free)

150

sieve
bowl
2 flat plates
kitchen towel
sharp knife
chopping board
tablespoon
tin opener
packet of wooden cocktail sticks

Snap To It!

1 Place a strawberry on the chopping board and carefully cut out the green stalk and the core with the sharp knife.

2 Place the strawberries in a sieve, hold it under the tap and and run cold water over the strawberries to wash them.

3 Shake the strawberries well to drain them and tip them on to some kitchen towel to dry off a bit.

4 Pull the grapes off the stalks, pop them into the sieve and wash them the same as the strawberries.

5 Open the tin of fruit. Place the sieve over the bowl and tip in the contents of the tin. The bowl will catch the juice which you can drink later. Leave the fruit to drain for a couple of minutes.

6 Using the tablespoon, lift the drained fruit on to the plate.

7 Thread the fruit on to the cocktail sticks in the same order as a traffic light and set on a clean plate.

8 Pour the yoghurt into a nice serving bowl and serve it with your Traffic Lights as a delicious dip.

Be a Crafty Croc

Try other fruits you like – you could make all sorts of different traffic light fruity sticks.

Vegetable Traffic Lights

These tasty treats are perfect for parties and barbecues! They are so simple and can be made with lots of vegetables – as long as they are the right colour!

Crafty Croc reckons that once you get the hang of it, you will be able to invent lots of your own. Check out his ideas at the end of the recipe.

Serves lots of friends

Takes 30 mins

No cooking

DB

(DF)

GF

(V)

VG

WF

You Will Need

1 small tub cherry tomatoes
1 cucumber
1 orange/yellow pepper

Dip
tub of humus
or 1 tbsp tomato ketchup)
or 1 tbsp natural yoghurt (low fat)

chopping board
sharp knife
sieve
2 flat plates
kitchen towel
packet of wooden cocktail sticks

Snap To It!

1 Tip the tomatoes into the sieve and wash them under cold running water for a few minutes.

2 Shake the tomatoes well to drain them and tip them on to some kitchen towel to dry off a bit.

3 Wash the cucumber in cold water, dry with some more kitchen towel and place on the chopping board.

4 Use the sharp knife to cut the cucumber into chunks about the same size as the cherry tomatoes. Set on the plate with the tomatoes.

5 Wash the pepper in cold running water, dry with kitchen towel and place on the chopping board.

6 Use the sharp knife to cut round the green stalk and core to remove them. You will find that the core has lots of little seeds – remove all these and then cut the orange pepper into squares about the size of the tomatoes and cucumber.

7 Thread the pieces of vegetable on to the cocktail sticks just like traffic lights and put onto a clean plate.

Be a Crafty Croc

Try other vegetable combinations – baby onions, little pieces of your favourite lettuce, cooked baby new potatoes – have a go.

Enjoy other dips – there are loads of ready-made dips in the chill cabinet for you to try – have a food adventure!!!

- **Dairy Free** and **Vegan** – use dairy-free yoghurt.

Spiky Hedgehog

This is an easy snack which looks great and everyone will find something they like. Don't worry if you don't have all the ingredients listed below – they are here just to give ideas for

food on a stick
that's tasty and quick!

This recipe can be adapted to any diet. Do not use cheese if you want to make this a **dairy-free** recipe, and no meat for **vegetarians**.

You Will Need

½ a melon
edam or cheddar cheese
cucumber
packet of sliced ham (or chicken or quorn)
2 fresh mandarine oranges
(or a small tin of pineapple chunks in fruit juice)
jar of pickled onions
1 banana
1 apple
dates
seedless grapes, washed and dried
cherry tomatoes, washed and dried

Dip
1 small carton of fromage frais (or soya yoghurt)
2 tbsp tomato ketchup
dash of Worcester sauce (or HP sauce)

large bowl
small bowl
chopping board
sharp knife
fork
tin opener
sieve
large plate
tablespoon
small plates or saucers
packet of wooden cocktail sticks

Snap To It!

1   Place the melon on the chopping board and carefully chop it in
    half. The skin will be quite tough so you may need to ask an
    adult to help. There's no point in risking a nasty cut.

2   Take one half of melon and use the spoon to scoop out the melon
    flesh. Put the flesh in a bowl for later – you only need the skin for
    this recipe.

3   Wash and dry the chopping board.

4   Now to prepare your bits 'n' pieces. Cut them all on the chopping
    board and then put the pieces on separate plates:

    cheese: using the sharp knife, carefully slice the cheese into 2cm
    (1 inch) slices. Cut the slices into squares. Put these on a plate.

    cucumber: cut this in half and then carefully cut into slices about
    0.5cm wide. Cut these slices in half and put on a plate.

    ham or chicken: carefully cut the slices into half and then roll the
    strips up.

    mandarine oranges and pineapple chunks: if you are using fresh
    mandarines, just peel them and separate the segments. If you have
    tinned mandarines, open the tin, hold a sieve over the small bowl
    and pour the fruit into the sieve to drain it. Place the drained fruit
    on a plate. Drain the pineapple in the same way and put it on
    another plate.

pickled onions: lift out 7 or 8 onions with a fork and place them on a plate.

banana: peel and slice the banana into thick slices.

apple: wash and dry the apple. Carefully slice it and then cut the slices into squares. Put them on a plate.

5   Put the grapes and cherry tomatoes on two other plates.

6   Open the packet of cocktail sticks and now you are ready to make your hedgehog!

7   Place the melon cut side down on the large plate so that it looks like a hump.

8   Take your cocktail sticks and spear on tomatoes, onions, pineapple pieces – anything you want in any order!

Go crazy! You can make vegetarian sticks and sticks with no cheese for people who can't eat dairy foods. Make whatever you want! Put three or four items on to each stick – choose flavours you thinks will taste good together, like ham, date and grape or cheese, pineapple and cucumber.

9   Leave about half of the stick empty so that you can hold it easily. Then, when you make each stick, spear it into the melon skin. Try to make enough sticks to cover the whole skin so that your melon looks like a hedgehog!

10   Enjoy with lots of friends!

Be a Crafty Croc

Mix the juice from the tinned mandarines and pineapple with some lemonade or fizzy water to make a refreshing drink to serve with your Hedgehog!

Pop it on a Pizza!

Have you ever thought about making your own pizza? Invite your friends and have loads of fun some rainy day – have a Pizza Making Party.

This is what to do . . .

1 Invite your friends – ask them to bring an apron and wear old clothes.

2 Each guest needs a large circle (bigger than the pizza base) of baking parchment. Get a dinner plate, place it on the baking parchment and draw round it. Cut out the circle with the scissors. Give each person a circle and ask them to write their name along the edge of it.

3 Everyone must now go and wash their hands, tie back any long hair and roll up your sleeves – it's Pizza Time!

You Will Need

aprons for everyone
baking parchment or greaseproof paper
dinner plates (larger than the pizza bases)
scissors
pencils
baking trays
fish slice
oven gloves
lots of small bowls (disposable ones are ideal)
plenty of spoons (disposable ones)
grater
3 large bowls

Serves 8

Takes as long as it takes!

Cook – oven

DB

(DF)

(GF)

(V)

(VG)

(WF)

Allow one pizza base for each person
(or you can use pitta bread)

In large bowls put . . .

1 bottle or carton of **passatta**
(this is sieved fresh tomatoes and is found beside the
pasta or Italian sauces in supermarkets)

grated **cheese** (low fat)
(edam is great as it becomes stringy when it melts,
giving a real Italian effect!)

fresh **basil**
(supermarkets have fresh plants and packets)

Put some or all of the following foods in the small bowls . . .

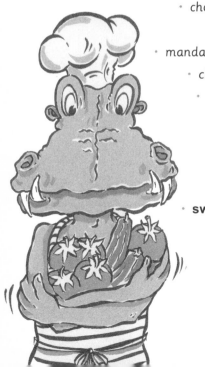

· chopped **pineapple** – drained ·

· sliced **tomatoes** ·

· mandarine **oranges** – tinned, drained ·

· chopped or sliced **peppers** ·

· chopped **spring onions** ·

· sliced **mushrooms** ·

· sliced **bananas** ·

· chopped **ham** ·

· flaked **tuna** ·

· **sweetcorn** – tinned, drained ·

· chopped **chicken** ·

· **anchovies** ·

· pitted **olives** ·

· sliced **pepperoni** ·

Snap To It!

1 Heat the oven to Gas 6, 400°F or 200°C.

2 Use the roughest side of the grater to grate the cheese into one of the large bowls. Be careful of your fingers, as the grater can be very sharp.

3 Put the passatta into the other large bowl.

4 Give each of your friends a pizza base or pitta bread to lay on their circle of paper. Get them to spread the top of the pizza or pitta with a spoon of passatta.

5 Choose as many fillings from the small bowls as you like and pile on top of the pizza base. Make faces and other designs.

6 Top the pizzas with a few torn basil leaves and some grated cheese.

7 Taking turns, lift your pizzas (and paper) on to the baking trays.

8 Use the oven gloves to put the trays in the oven. Bake for about 10 to 15 minutes until the cheese is melted, bubbling and starting to brown.

9 Wearing oven gloves, lift the tray from the oven and set on a heat-resistant surface. Use the fish slice to carefully lift the pizza on to the serving plate.

Be a Clever Croc

Read the names on the baking parchment and it will help you to give each person their own pizza.

Wheat Free and **Gluten Free** – you can now buy ready-made gluten and wheat free pizza bases. Remember to bake them on a separate tray.

Dairy Free and **Vegans** – miss out the cheese.

Pick a Pack of Puff Pastry!

You can put lots of different fillings inside puff pastry to make all sorts of delicious goodies. Here are some suggestions, but you can experiment with your own ideas too!

Marmite Munchies

You will need to use special pastry if you want to make this a **Gluten** or **Wheat Free** recipe.

Makes 30–34

Takes 45 mins

Cook – oven

DB

DF

(GF)

V

VG

(WF)

You Will Need

110g (4oz) puff pastry
½ small jar Marmite
sunflower oil (use an oil spray if you have it)
flour
water

rolling pin
palette knife or fish slice
baking tray
sharp knife
knife for spreading
kitchen towel
plate
oven gloves

Snap To It !

1 Arrange the shelves in the oven so the baking tray can sit on the middle shelf. Turn on the oven to heat at Gas 7, 425F or 240°C.

2 Sprinkle some flour on to a clean surface and roll out the pastry with the rolling pin to make a rectangle about 25 x 30cm (10 x 12 inches).

3 Mix the Marmite with a little water and then use the knife to spread it very thinly over the pastry.

4 Starting at the shorter edge of the rectangle, roll up the pastry tightly, like a Swiss roll.

5 Carefully lift it on to a plate, making sure the join is underneath, and chill for 15 minutes in the fridge.

6 While the roll is chilling, drop a little sunflower oil on the baking tray and rub it all over the tray with some clean kitchen towel.

7 Take the roll out of the fridge and use the sharp knife to cut it into slices about 5mm (¼ inch) wide.

8 Lay these pieces flat on the greased tray, pressing them down gently with the palm of your hand.

9 Using the oven gloves, put the baking tray in the oven. Bake for 10 to 15 minutes until puffed and golden.

10 Use the oven gloves to take the tray out of the oven and set it on a heat-resistant surface.

11 Use the palette knife to place the Munchies on the plate.

12 Serve while still warm. Marmite Munchies can be stored in an airtight box for up to 1 week. Re-heat for 5 minutes in the oven at Gas 4, 350°F or 180°C. Remember to use oven gloves!

Be a Crafty Croc

If you like anchovies, try spreading the pastry with a very thin coating of anchovy paste instead of Marmite. Try pesto or sun-dried tomato puree as well.

Tomato Twisters

Makes 32

Takes 45 mins

Cook – oven

DB

(DF)

(GF)

(V)

VG

(WF)

Crafty Croc likes to serve these Tomato Twisters when his friends come round. Your friends will love them too! You can eat them as they are, or try them dipped in creamy humus or Guacamole For All (see page 91).

You will need to use special pastry if you want to make this a **Gluten** or **Wheat Free** recipe. For a **Dairy Free** or **Vegan** recipe, miss out the cheese.

You Will Need

110g (4oz) puff pastry
1 tbsp tomato ketchup
1 tbsp cheese
flour
sunflower oil

bowl
rolling pin
grater
plate
knife for spreading
baking tray
chopping board
sharp knife
kitchen towel
oven gloves

Snap To It !

1 Arrange the shelves in the oven so the baking tray can sit on the middle shelf. Turn on the oven to heat at Gas 7, 450°F or 240°C.

2 Sprinkle some flour on to a clean surface and roll out the pastry with the rolling pin to make a rectangle about 25 x 30cm (10 x 12 inches). Cut this piece in half.

3 Use the roughest side of the grater to grate the cheese into the bowl. Be careful of your fingers, as the grater can be very sharp.

4 Carefully lift one pastry half on to the chopping board and use the knife to spread it with the ketchup.

5 Sprinkle the grated cheese on top.

6 Place the other half of pastry on top to make a sandwich. Roll the top with the rolling pin to press the pastry together.

7 Cut the pastry into 16 strips. Then cut each strip in half so you have 32 strips.

8 Twist each piece several times to make twisty shapes.

9 Drop a little sunflower oil on the baking tray and rub it all over the tray with some clean kitchen towel.

10 Lay the twists on the greased baking tray, making sure you leave enough room around them to spread.

11 Using the oven gloves, carefully place the baking tray in the oven. Bake for 10 to 15 minutes until puffed and golden.

12 Use the oven gloves to take the tray out of the oven and set it on a heat-resistant surface to cool of a few minutes.

13 Serve warm. If you don't manage to eat them all, your Tomato Twisters can be stored in an airtight container for up to 1 week. Re-heat for 5 minutes on a baking tray in the oven at Gas 4, 350°F or 180°C. Remember to use oven gloves!

Roll Up, Roll Up!

Makes 48

No cooking

Takes 10 mins

DB

VG

Just the snack to make for a party.

Crafty Croc is sure your friends will queue up for these bite-size treats. This is his favourite party recipe and it makes plenty for everyone!

You Will Need

2 eggs
2oz (50g) cheese
1 dessertspoon mayonnaise
1 dessertspoon fromage frais
(or natural yoghurt)
large pack of cherry tomatoes
12 thin slices bread
salt + pepper (to taste)

small pan
chopping board
bowl
grater
plate
knife
fork
plastic container
cocktail sticks

Snap To It!

1 Place the eggs into the pan and pour in enough water to cover them. Turn up the heat to medium and let the eggs boil for 10 minutes. Turn off the heat.

2 Carefully lift the pan into the sink and put it under the cold tap. Run cold water slowly into the pan for about 4 or 5 minutes. This will help cool the hard-boiled eggs.

3 Carefully grate the cheese on to a plate.

4 Take one of the eggs and roll it along the table to crack the shell. Peel off the shell and wash the egg under cold running water. Do the same with the other eggs.

5 Put the eggs in a bowl and mash them with the back of a fork.

6 Add the grated cheese, mayonnaise, fromage frais, salt and pepper. Mix them all together with the fork.

7 Place the bread on the chopping board and cut off the crusts with the knife.

8 Divide the eggy mixture between the slices of bread and spread it out to the edges with the knife.

9 Starting at the shorter edge of one slice, roll it up, press together gently and secure with 2 cocktail sticks. Do the same with the other slices.

10 Put the rolls into a plastic container and chill for 1 hour.

11 Place the chilled rolls on the chopping board. Cut each roll into four and spear each one with a cocktail stick.

12 Carefully stick a cherry tomato on to each cocktail stick and slide it down carefully until it is just resting on the roll.

13 Pile all the rolls on to a plate and serve.

Be a Crafty Croc

Don't leave eggs in hot water or they will go rubbery and the yolk will turn a funny grey-black colour. Yuk!

Tasty Taco Treats !

Serves 6

Takes 15 mins

No cooking

DB

(DF)

GF

(V)

(VG)

WF

These delicious spicy Mexican crisp treats are just made for mouth-watering fillings and you can choose and make them all yourself. Invite some friends to share – it's great fun!

No cooking needed – this is an anytime party for a wet day!

You Will Need

2 packets of ready-made taco shells
bag of salad leaves
ripe avocado pear – peeled, chopped
a little lemon juice
4 tomatoes – chopped
grated carrot
grated apple
6 spring onions – peeled and chopped
small tin Mexicorn (sweetcorn and peppers)
selection of spiced cold meats
sardines in spring water – drained
tub coleslaw
raisins

Dressing
1 small carton natural yoghurt
(or soya yoghurt)
2 tbsp tomato ketchup
1 tsp chilli powder
1 tbsp mayonnaise (or egg-free alternative)
(or a ready-made dressing)

lots of small bowls (disposable dishes are great)
spoons (use plastic ones)
dinner plates
napkins
salad bowl and servers
tin opener
tablecloth (plastic if possible)
large plate

Snap To It!

1 Cover the table with the large plastic tablecloth.

2 Make the dressing: Mix the yoghurt, tomato ketchup, chilli powder and mayonnaise in a clean bowl. Stick in a spoon and put the bowl on the table.

3 Prepare the avocado, tomatoes, carrot, apple and spring onions (see pages 10 to 14).

4 Put each of the ingredients into their own small dish with a spoon. (Mix a little lemon juice with the avocado to stop it turning black.)

5 Put the salad into a large bowl with the servers.

6 Arrange all the dishes in the middle of the table.

7 Lay the tacos on the large plate and put this on the table.

8 Now! Seat your guests round the table. Give everyone a napkin and a dinner plate. Hand round the tacos – each person can fill their own taco from the fillings on the table, top with a dollop of dressing and enjoy!

Be a Crafty Croc

Why not make one of the exciting drinks from the Thirst Quenchers chapter (page 91) to make the party go with a fizz!! Remember, you don't have to stop at these fillings – try any of the other exciting ones in this book.

Spicy Bites with Cool Dip

You Will Need

Spicy Bites
2oz (50g) chopped red peppers
1 onion
1 tbsp sunflower oil
1 lb (450g) courgettes
2 large carrots
½ tsp ground cumin
2 eggs
1 tsp salt
ground black pepper
4oz (110g) fresh breadcrumbs
plate of dry breadcrumbs to coat
sunflower oil to deep fry

Tomato Dip
4 tbsp tomato ketchup
2 tbsp fromage frais (or soya yoghurt)
½ tsp chilli powder

deep-fat pan or deep-fat fryer
frying pan
baking tray
chopping board
sharp knife
kitchen towel
2 bowls
grater
fork
small dish
wooden spoon
draining spoon
cocktail sticks

Makes 25

Takes 1 hour

Cook – hob and
deep fry (or oven)

Snap To It !

1   Mix the tomato ketchup with the fromage frais (or natural yoghurt) and the chilli powder in the small dish.

2   Peel the onion and place it on the chopping board. Carefully use the sharp knife to cut it in half. Take one half, place the flat side down and carefully cut the onion into slices. Then cut across these slices to make small squares.

3   Wash the pepper in cold running water, dry with kitchen towel and place on the chopping board.

4   Use the sharp knife to cut round the green stalk and core to remove them. Remove all the little seeds and then cut the pepper in half. Take one half, place the flat side down and carefully cut the pepper into slices. Then cut across these slices to make small squares about the size of the onion.

5   Put a tablespoon of sunflower oil into the pan. Add the onion and pepper pieces.

6   Place the frying pan on the hob and turn the heat to medium. Cook the onion and pepper until very soft but not coloured.

7   Remove the pan from the heat and set on a heat-resistant surface.

8   Wash and dry the courgette. Use the roughest side of the grater to grate the courgette into the bowl. Be careful of your fingers, as the grater can be very sharp.

9   Wash and peel the carrot. Use the roughest side of the grater to grate the carrot into the bowl with the courgette. Be careful of your fingers, as the grater can be very sharp.

10   Add the courgettes and carrots to the fried onion and pepper.

11   Add the cumin.

12   Holding the handle in one hand, use the other hand to stir with the wooden spoon.

13   Break the eggs one by one into a clean bowl. Add the salt and pepper and beat well with the fork.

14   Add the breadcrumbs to the egg mixture.

Turn the page . . .

15 Using the wooden spoon, scrape out all of the vegetable mixture from the pan into the eggs and mix together.

16 Take a little of the mixture into your hands and make into balls about the size of a walnut. (If you wet your hands before starting, the mixture will not stick to them.)

17 Roll the ball in the dry breadcrumbs on the plate.

18 Do the same with the rest of the mixture.

19 Put 4 sheets of kitchen towel on a baking tray and place it beside the cooker.

20 Fill the deep-fat pan with sunflower oil up to the oil mark and place on a medium heat, or switch on the deep-fat fryer and let it heat.

21 Test the temperature of the oil. When the oil is read, gently lower the balls into the oil using a frying basket or the draining spoon. Stand back so the hot oil does not splash and burn you.

22 Deep fry the balls for about 4 minutes until they are golden.

23 Using the frying basket or draining spoon to carefully lift the balls out of the oil. Place them on the kitchen towel to drain.

24 Spear each of the balls with cocktail sticks.

25 Serve hot with the tomato dip.

Be a Crafty Croc

You can *bake* the Spicy Balls in the oven instead of deep-frying them. Heat the oven to Gas 6, 400°F or 200°C. Put the Spicy Balls on a baking tray and use oven gloves to put the tray in the oven. Bake for 30 minutes or until golden. Use oven gloves to lift the tray out of the oven and set it on a heat-resistant surface.

To make these Spicy Bites **Wheat Free** and **Gluten Free**, use special bread to make the breadcrumbs.

Jolly Jellies

See how many silly sweeties you can think of to put into the jelly!

This is a great recipe for a party – depending on the sweets you choose, you can play 'hunt the blue sweet' and 'who has the spider?'

Serves 6

Takes 2 hours

No cooking

(DF)

GF

WF

You Will Need

1 red jelly
1 green jelly
packet of jelly sweets of your choice

2 bowls or heat-proof measuring jug
old yoghurt tubs (washed) or individual dishes
wooden spoon

Snap To It!

1 Prepare a green jelly and a red jelly as it says on the packet.

2 Pour a layer of green jelly into the foot of the tubs or dishes and put them into the fridge or freezer to set.

3 Lay a few small jelly sweets on to the set jelly.

4 Pour over some red jelly and put back into the fridge or freezer. Continue making layers of jelly and sweets until the dish is full.

5 Serve chilled on its own or with a dollop of ice cream or fromage frais.

Christmas Dinner Jackets

Serves 4

Takes 1 hour

Cook – hob and oven

DB

(DF)

(GF)

(V)

(VG)

(WF)

Christmas is the time for wrapping presents and gifts – now you can wrap up your food too!

You can make these Christmas Dinner Jackets in advance and then re-heat them in the oven.

For an even simpler recipe, buy pre-cooked baby potatoes.

You Will Need

450g pack of baby boiling potatoes
2 tsp salt
110g (4oz) cooked turkey (or chicken)
2 tbsp sweetcorn
cranberry sauce or jelly (or gravy)
gravy
left-over stuffing
grated edam cheese

deep saucepan + lid
sharp knife
chopping board
colander
foil
scissors
bowl
tablespoon

Snap To It !

1 Wash the potatoes and put them in the deep saucepan.

2 Add the salt and place the pan on the hob. Turn the heat to high. Bring to the boil and put the lid on the pan.

3 Turn down the heat to low and cook for 20 minutes until tender.

4 Place a colander in the sink and turn on the cold tap (this will get rid of the steam). Pour the potatoes into the colander to drain. Leave them to cool until you can handle them.

5 Use the scissors to cut a square of foil which will cover the bottom of the potato, like a dinner jacket or kilt! Cut enough squares of foil so that there is one for each potato.

6 Prepare the filling:

   a) Finely chop some left-over turkey or chicken into the bowl.

   b) Add a little cranberry jelly or turkey gravy to moisten.

   c) The rest is up to you! Add sweetcorn for crunch. Add some leftover stuffing too if you like. Mix with the tablespoon

   d) Sprinkle everything with some grated edam.

7 Place a potato on the chopping board. With a sharp knife, carefully split the potato almost in half, top to bottom, but don't cut all the way through.

8 Fill the split potato with a spoonful of the filling.

9 Wrap the base of the potato in a square of foil so that the bottom is covered but the filling can be seen. The foil will help the potato halves to stay together.

10 Cut, fill and wrap all the potatoes.

To re-heat your potatoes in the oven

Heat the oven to Gas 6, 400°F or 200°C. Place all the foil wrapped potatoes on a baking tray. Use oven gloves to put the tray in the oven. Cook for 20 minutes. Remember to use oven gloves to lift out the tray and set it on a heat-resistant surface. Serve.

I love these crispy Christmas dippers and I bet you will too!

Rudolph's Rednose Dippers with Cranberry Sauce

Makes about
40 meat balls

Takes 45 mins

Cook – oven

DB

DF

(GF)

(WF)

You Will Need

For the Dippers
12oz (335g) minced turkey meat
4oz (110g) pork sausage meat
3oz (75g) fresh breadcrumbs
salt and pepper
(1 egg – beaten)
sunflower oil

For the Sauce
1 jar cranberry sauce

bowl
fork
baking tray
kitchen towel
food tongs
cocktail sticks
oven gloves

Snap To It!

1 Arrange the shelves in the oven so the baking tray can sit on the middle shelf. Turn on the oven to heat at Gas 5, 375F or 190°C.

2 Drop a little sunflower oil on the baking tray and rub it all over the tray with some clean kitchen towel.

3 Put all the ingredients for the dippers into a large bowl and mix them well together with the fork.

4 Season well with salt and pepper and mix.

5 If the mixture is a little stiff, add some beaten egg and mix it well together.

6 Lift some of the mixture in your hands and shape it into a small balls about the size of a walnut. Place it on to the oiled baking tray.

7 Do the same with the rest of the mixture until it is all used up.

8 Using the oven gloves, carefully place the tray in the oven and leave to bake for about 15 minutes.

9 Put on the oven gloves and carefully remove the tray from the oven and set on a heat-resistant surface. Use the food tongs to turn the balls over.

10 Still using the oven gloves, put the tray back in the oven and bake for another 15 minutes until golden.

11 Carefully — remember your oven gloves! — remove the tray from the oven and set on a heat-resistant surface.

12 Spear each ball with a cocktail stick and serve warm with the cranberry sauce.

Be a Crafty Croc

If you think that the cranberry sauce is too thick, thin it down with a little boiled water.
Try other sauces, like tomato, or chutneys. Be adventurous!

Crisp Cinnamon Sticks

Makes 20

Takes 45 mins

Cook – oven

DF

V

VG

Crispy, crunchy
Hot or cold
Eat them freshly baked.
Not so tasty cold!

You Will Need

10 slices of white bread
3oz (75g) sunflower oil
2oz (50g) castor sugar
2 tsp ground cinnamon

chopping board
sharp knife
cling film
rolling pin
baking tray
small bowl
teaspoon
pastry brush
cocktail sticks
oven gloves

Snap To It!

1   Arrange the shelves in the oven so the baking tray can sit on the middle shelf. Turn on the oven to heat at Gas 6, 400°F or 200°C.

2   Place a slice of bread on the chopping board and cut round the edges with a sharp knife to remove the crusts.

3   Place a slice of bread between two sheets of cling film and roll it out thinly with the rolling pin.

4   Remove the cling film and use the pastry brush to brush each side of the slice with the sunflower oil.

5   Mix the sugar and ground cinnamon together in a small bowl.

6   Sprinkle the sugar mixture over one side of the bread.

7   Roll up the slice from the narrow end to make a small Swiss roll.

8   Trim off each end of the roll to make it neater and then cut the roll in half. Secure each half with a cocktail stick.

9   Repeat steps 2 to 8 with all the other slices of bread.

10 Place all the rolls on a baking tray and use the oven gloves to carefully put the tray in the oven. Bake for 20 to 30 minutes until crisp and golden.

11 Use oven gloves to remove the tray from the oven and set on a heat-resistant surface. Leave to cool.

12 Carefully remove the sticks and serve. You can eat them warm or cool, but be sure to eat them the same day – they taste better.

Be a Crafty Croc

Try dipping the Cinnamon Sticks into your favourite flavour of creamy yoghurt (or soya yoghurt).

Dress Up the Fruit

Fruit never looked so fab!

A mix of small fruit pieces will look great on the plate and will give your tongue a real treat!

You Will Need

Small fruit pieces
clementine segments, strawberries, mandarine segments, apple slices, grapes or dates

bar of chocolate

saucepan
cocktail sticks
pyrex bowl
greaseproof paper or foil
baking tray
oven gloves

Snap To It!

1 Line a baking tray with the greaseproof paper or foil.

2 Break the chocolate bar into the pyrex bowl. Now to melt it –

ON THE HOB

a) Half fill the saucepan with water and place it on the hob.

b) Turn the heat to high and bring the water to boil, then turn down the heat to low.

c) Carefully use the oven gloves to place the bowl over the pan of hot water. (Make sure the water is not touching the bottom of the bowl.) Let the chocolate melt.

d) Turn the heat off and place the pan on a heat-resistant surface. Use the oven gloves to carefully lift the bowl out of the pan.

IN THE MICROWAVE

a) Place the bowl of broken chocolate in the microwave. Cook on high for 1 minute.

b) Use oven gloves to remove the bowl. Stir the chocolate and put the bowl back in the microwave – use your oven gloves!

c) Microwave for another minute and the chocolate will have melted. Use the oven gloves to carefully lift the bowl out of the microwave and set it on a heat-resistant surface.

3 Spear each piece of fruit with a cocktail stick then dip the fruit into the chocolate enough to cover about half of the piece of fruit.

4 Lay the chocolate coated fruit on the baking tray and leave in a cool place to set.

5 Serve on a pretty plate. Store in a cool place if you want to keep them for a few hours, but eat them the same day.

Be a Clever Croc

Only use firm, dry fruit and eat the day you make it.

• **Dairy Free** or **Vegan** – use chocolate which is suitable for dairy-free or vegan diets.

Cinnamon Dipped Fruits

Dipping's all the rage, so be cool this Yule!

Makes 12

Takes 10 mins

No cooking

(DB)

(DF)

GF

(V)

VG

WF

You Will Need

12 fl.oz (350ml) Greek style natural yoghurt
(or fromage frais)
1 tbsp soft brown sugar
1 tsp ground cinnamon
pinch ground ginger
pinch grated nutmeg

Fruits
1 punnet of strawberries
1 small tin of pineapple chunks
2 apples – Cox's or Braeburn
3 mandarines

large bowl
wooden spoon
teaspoon
tablespoon
cocktail sticks
flat plate
fancy dish
sieve
sharp knife
chopping board
tin opener

Snap To It!

1. Pour the yoghurt into the bowl and add the sugar and spices (cinnamon, ginger and nutmeg).

2. Mix well together with the wooden spoon and then pour into the fancy serving dish.

3. Place a strawberry on the chopping board and carefully cut out the green stalk and the core with the sharp knife.

4. Do the same with the rest of the strawberries.

5. Place the strawberries in a sieve, hold it under the tap and run cold water over the strawberries to wash them. Drain them well.

6. Thread one strawberry on to each of the cocktail sticks. Place them on the flat plate.

7. Peel the mandarines and remove any white stringy bits.

8. Pull the segments apart and thread the pieces on to the cocktail sticks. Place them on the flat plate.

9. Place the sieve over a bowl and tip the pineapple chunks into it. The bowl will collect the juice which you can drink later.

10. Thread the pineapple chunks on to the cocktail sticks. Place them on the flat plate.

11. Wash and dry the apples. Place one on the chopping board and carefully cut it into four pieces using the sharp knife. Then carefully cut out the core from each quarter. Do the same with the other apples.

12. Cut the apples into chunks and put them on the cocktail sticks.

13. Serve on a clean plate and have fun dipping your fruits into the delicious creamy yoghurt.

Be a Crafty Croc

For a **Dairy Free** or **Vegan** recipe, use soya yoghurt for the dip.

Diabetics would be better not to add sugar to the dip.

Christmas Jewels

Impress your family and friends with these colourful treats! They take a little time to make, but they are worth every minute.

Put the boiled sweets in a sealed poly bag and bash them with rolling pin to break them up.

The best fun is at the end when you thread the ribbon through the small holes in the biscuits and hang them on the Christmas tree!

You Will Need

8oz (225g) plain flour (gluten or wheat free)
4oz butter (or dairy-free margarine)
4oz castor sugar
1 level tsp baking powder
1 level tsp ground cinnamon
1 egg, beaten
boiled sweets (broken into pieces)

baking tray
baking parchment or greaseproof paper
large mixing bowl
wooden spoon
rolling pin
2.5cm (4 inch) round pastry cutter
smaller pastry cutters
skewer
oven gloves
thin ribbon

Snap To It !

1. Arrange the shelves in the oven so the baking tray can sit on the middle shelf. Turn on the oven to heat at Gas 5, 375°F or 190°C.

2. Line the baking tray with baking parchment or oiled greaseproof paper.

3. Put the butter and sugar into the mixing bowl and beat well together with the wooden spoon (this is called 'creaming' – see page 20) until the mixture is fluffy.

4. Add the flour, baking powder and cinnamon.

5. Pour in the egg and mix well with the wooden spoon.

6. Take the wooden spoon out of the bowl – its time to get your hands in! Knead the mixture so that it comes together in a ball.

7. Place the ball of dough on a clean, floured surface and use the rolling pin to roll it out to about 3mm (⅛ inch) thick.

8. Use the pastry cutter to cut out rounds about 4 inches (2.5cms) in diameter.

9. When you have cut out as many rounds as you can, knead the dough together and then roll it out again so you can cut more rounds. Keep cutting and kneading and rolling until you have used up all the dough.

10. Use a skewer to make a hole at one end of each of the rounds about 1cm (½ inch) from the edge.

11. Choose a smaller cutter to cut some holes in each of the rounds.

12. Lift the rounds on to the baking tray and use oven gloves to put the tray in the oven. Bake for 7 minutes.

13. Use the oven gloves to lift the tray out of the oven and set it on a heat-resistant surface. Leave to cool for a few minutes.

14. Carefully place pieces of boiled sweets in the holes and use the oven gloves to put the tray back in the oven. Bake for 5 to 8 minutes until the sweets have melted and the biscuits are crisp.

15. Use the oven gloves to lift the tray out of the oven and set it on a heat-resistant surface. Leave to cool on the baking tray.

16. Carefully thread ribbon though the hole in the top of the biscuit.

Mincemeat Crumbles

This recipe is much simpler than all the fuss of making individual mincemeat pies, and they taste extremely good indeed!!

This recipe (and the next one for Mincemeat Flapjacks) can be made by **Wheat Frees**, **Vegetarians** and **Vegans** so long as you check the type of mincemeat you use.

You Will Need

335g (12oz) plain flour
160g (6oz) margarine (dairy free)
110g (4oz) castor sugar
450g (1lb) mincemeat (wheat free or vegan)
icing sugar to dust
sunflower oil

baking tin
(20 x 28cm or 8 x12 inches)
mixing bowl
tablespoon
wooden spoon
knife for spreading
kitchen towel
oven gloves

Snap To It!

1 Arrange the shelves in the oven so the baking tin can sit on the middle shelf. Turn on the oven to heat at Gas 4, 350°F or 180°C.

2 Drop a little sunflower oil on the baking tin and rub it all over the tin with some clean kitchen towel.

3 Put the flour into the mixing bowl.

4 Add the margarine.

5 Using the knife, roughly chop up the margarine into pieces.

6 Using your fingertips, rub the margarine into the flour until it mixes together and looks like fine breadcrumbs.

7 Add the castor sugar and stir well together with the wooden spoon.

8 Sprinkle half the mixture over the base of the tin and press down lightly with the back of a tablespoon.

5 Spread the mincemeat over the top. Use the knife to spread it evenly to the edges.

6 Sprinkle the rest of the flour mixture over the top. Press down lightly with the back of the tablespoon.

7 Use the oven gloves to place the tin in the oven. Bake for 45 to 50 minutes until firm and golden.

8 Using oven gloves, carefully lift out the tin from the oven and place it on a heat-resistant surface. Leave to cool in the tin.

9 Use the knife to cut the mixture into 18 pieces.

10 Shake over a little icing sugar and serve.

Be a Crafty Croc

These taste great with a dollop of ice cream! (**Dairy free** if necessary.)

185

Marvellous Mincemeat Flapjacks

Makes 12 to
16 biscuits

Takes 1 hour

Cook – hob
(or microwave)
and oven

(DF)

(V)

(VG)

(WF)

Mincemeat pies first appeared at Christmas during the reign of Elizabeth I. In those days, the mincemeat was made from a mixture of minced mutton or beef and fruits and spices! It was said if you ate 12 mincemeat pies between Christmas day and Twelfth Night the New Year would be one of Good Fortune.

Mincemeat pies take a while to make so try this recipe instead – Flapjacks are quick to make and delicious to eat.

You Will Need

3oz (75g) margarine (dairy-free)
2oz (50g) soft brown sugar
7oz porridge oats
4oz (110g) mincemeat (wheat free or vegan)
sunflower oil

baking tin about 20cm (8 inches) square
small bowl or small saucepan
large bowl
wooden spoon
kitchen towel
sharp knife
palette knife
plate
oven gloves

Snap To It !

1 Arrange the shelves in the oven so the baking tin can sit on the middle shelf. Turn on the oven to heat at Gas 5, 375°F or 190°C.

2 Drop a little sunflower oil on the baking tin and rub it all over the tin with some clean kitchen towel.

3 Decide how to melt the margarine and sugar.

   ### IN THE MICROWAVE

   a) Put the margarine and sugar into the small bowl.

   b) Place the bowl in the microwave and cook for 1 minute on high power to melt the margarine and sugar.

   c) Put on the oven gloves and take the bowl from the microwave.

   ### ON THE HOB

   a) Put the margarine and sugar into a small saucepan.

   b) Place the saucepan on in the hob and turn the heat to low. Stir with the wooden spoon all the time until it is melted, being careful not to burn the mixture.

   c) Lift the pan off the hob and set on a heat-resistant surface.

4 Use the wooden spoon to scrape the margarine and sugar mixture into the large mixing bowl.

5 Add all the other ingredients (flour, oats and mincemeat) and mix well together using the wooden spoon.

6 Use the wooden spoon to scrape the mixture into the baking tin and press it evenly into the tin.

7 Use oven gloves to place the tin in the the middle of the oven. bake for about 20 minutes. This burns easily so you must check it after 20 minutes. If the mixture turns golden, it is ready. If not, put it back in the oven for another 5 minutes.

8 Use the oven gloves to take the tin out of the oven and set it on a heat-resistant surface. Leave it to cool a little, then use the sharp knife to cut into squares.

9 When the tin is completely cold, use the palette knife to ease the squares on to a plate and serve. Tasting time is here!

Santa's Quick Shorties

Choose biscuits that are suitable for you and your friends' diets. Then impress them with these quick and easy tasty treats!

Makes about 24

Takes 30 mins

No cooking

(DF)

(GF)

(V)

VG

(WF)

You Will Need

packet of shortcake biscuits
jar of jam (high-fruit, low-sugar)
3 tbsp icing sugar
water
silver icing balls

small mixing bowl
spreading knife
tablespoon
teaspoon
plate

Snap To It!

1 Using the knife, spread jam on one side of a biscuit.

2 Place another biscuit on top to make a sandwich.

3 Do the same with the rest of the biscuits.

4 Put the icing sugar in the bowl and add a teaspoon of water, stirring with the tablespoon. Keep adding teaspoons of water while stirring until the icing turns smooth, like thick cream.

5 Drop a teaspoon of icing on top of the biscuit. Spread out using the back of the teaspoon and lay it on the plate.

6 Do the same with the rest of the biscuit sandwiches.

7 Make a festive pattern on top using the silver balls. Make stars . . . zig zags, you choose!

Index